ORAL LANGUAGE ACTIVITIES
FOR SPECIAL CHILDREN

Darlene Mannix

Illustrated by
Carolyn M. Quinton

The Center for Applied Research in Education, Inc.
West Nyack, N.Y.

© 1987 *by*
THE CENTER FOR APPLIED
RESEARCH IN EDUCATION, INC.

West Nyack, N.Y.

10 9 8 7 6 5

Most of the objectives used in this book have been adapted from the pragmatic objectives in the *Sequential Communication Objectives for Remediation* (SCOR) program by Jeannie Brown Barton, Janet Royer Lanza, and Carolyn Collard Wilson, published by LinguiSystems, Inc., Moline, Illinois, and are used by permission.

Library of Congress Cataloging-in-Publication Data

Oral language activities for special students

  1. Children—United States—language. 2. Learning
disabled children—Education—United States.
3. English language—Spoken English—United States—
Problems, exercises, etc. I. Title.
LB1139.L3M35⁴ 1986   371.9'044   86-24455

ISBN 0-87628-637-6

Printed in the United States of America

This book is affectionately dedicated to:

Kevin, Sam, Albert, Laura, Renee, Gary, Doug, Michael, Troy, Brian, and Ben

with special thanks to Jackie Garfield, Lois Brown, Maude Myrick, and Gerald Terrell at Rose Hill Elementary School in Charlottesville, Virginia

ABOUT THE AUTHOR

Darlene Mannix is currently a learning disabilities teacher in the South La Porte County Co-op, La Porte, Indiana, at South Central Elementary School and Wanatah Public School. She has also taught language-disordered, mentally retarded, multiply handicapped, and emotionally disturbed children.

Ms. Mannix received her Bachelor of Science degree from Taylor University and her Master's degree in Learning Disabilities from Indiana University. She is a member of the Council for Exceptional Children, and was a presenter at the 1984 Virginia CEC Convention. She is the author of the *Mannix Classroom Skills Curriculum*, to be published by ASIEP Education Company of Portland, Oregon.

THIS BOOK IS FOR...

1. the child who doesn't answer questions...

2. the child who needs help solving problems...

3. the child with nothing to say...

4. the child who needs practice with everyday oral language.

ABOUT THIS BOOK

Oral Language Activities for Special Children presents over 100 reproducible activities appropriate for elementary students, particularly those in special education. This book is designed to help you, the classroom teacher, provide activities that will promote awareness and practice in specific language skills. Most students become easily adept at practical language skills without specific instruction, but some children—especially those who are socially/developmentally delayed, learning disabled, or language disordered—have difficulty with these skills in everyday situations. It is for them that this book is written.

Practical language skills are important for all students to master so they can effectively communicate with others. This is particularly important in the classroom, where ideas are often shared verbally. Children who are unable to express themselves clearly are at a great disadvantage when they must answer questions or give their opinions. Likewise, children who have difficulty understanding oral language will experience problems in organizing their approach to situations presented orally. Some children may have difficulty understanding questions and their required responses. For example, "where" questions usually require a response that gives a location. A child who does not understand this may answer inappropriately without giving the information requested. Even a child with well-developed expressive language skills can have difficulty maintaining a conversation with others because of an inability to pick up on verbal cues to shift the topic, let others have a chance to talk, or terminate a conversation.

The activities can be used with an entire class or with just a few students. Some of the activities may call for written responses, but the intent of all the activities is to emphasize oral expression. The ready-to-use activities serve as a vehicle for discussion of, or practice in, a specific skill. You can record individual responses on the activity sheets and then discuss them within the groups. Although some of the activities involve reading, you can read the items aloud to students and help them record their responses to smooth the flow of the activities.

Oral Language Activities for Special Children is organized into four sections, each including at least 20 reproducible worksheet activities:

- Section I, "Activities to Help Students Understand and Respond to Questions," deals with students' experiences in asking and responding to questions. The 21 activity sheets in this section cover such topics as

"Should I Answer 'Yes' or 'No'?," "Tell Me About Yourself," and "Select the 'Where' Answer."

- Section II, "Activities to Help Students Improve Their Problem-solving Abilities," focuses on the students' verbal skills to express logical and reasonable answers to questions. The 29 activity pages in Section II include sequencing events, asking for additional information, and providing solutions.

- Section III, "Activities to Help Students Improve Their Conversational Skills," teaches students appropriate ways to begin, carry on, and end a conversation. The 27 activity sheets in this section include "Don't Leave Someone Out," "Keep Saying More," and "Stay on the Topic!"

- Section IV, "Activities to Help Students with Their Everyday Communication Skills," helps improve the students' daily exchanges of information with others, especially in situations that occur in the classroom. This section, offering 39 activity sheets, covers such topics as "Tell Me About It!," "On the Playground," and "How I Felt Today."

Practical goals and objectives are given for each section and activity, and it is helpful for the students to be aware of these. Each section also gives you at least one sample of a letter you can send home to parents that describes the content and activities in the particular section, as well as follow-up activities that can be done at home. At the end of each section is a collection of Enrichment Activities that further extend the skills you are reinforcing. A special feature of the book is the Skills Index, which will help you quickly locate all the activities for reinforcing and teaching a particular skill.

Although the content of all four sections is aimed primarily at school situations and needs, transference and generalization of skills can be provided for by slightly modifying the activity sheets or examples to meet other needs.

While a student may demonstrate difficulty with a language skill in all settings, *Oral Language Activities for Special Children* concentrates primarily on situations in a typical classroom or school setting. These are situations that you would encounter every day with your students, so by using meaningful activities as learning experiences, the students will be more likely to transfer the skills learned to any environment. You can thus "train" your students to develop skills that are observable throughout the school day. For this reason, it is important that you tune in to situations throughout the day in which you can continually provide these students with the chance to use the skills that you've identified and given them practice in, in class.

You may not have much direct control over the students' experiences outside school, but the activity pages and suggestions may have an indirect influence at home. Many parents are willing and even anxious to work with their children at home to improve their skills, and would appreciate suggestions from school. The letters to parents can be sent home to explain briefly the type of language skills and practice that will be addressed at school and give suggestions for incorporating these skills and techniques into the home.

Opportunity for language training exists continually throughout the day within the classroom, but setting aside a specific time for language skill training can help you organize materials and ensure that certain specific skills are covered. It can also help the student focus on mastery of a single skill by increasing his or her awareness of that skill as well as by providing concentrated practice in it. A suggestion: introduce each activity to the students by stating the general goal and specific objective to be worked on. The activity pages can then be distributed on a daily basis, and additional activities, such as the enrichment ideas at the end of each section, can be included if you wish to place more emphasis on a specific objective or want an alternative to the worksheet format.

Short sessions of language practice are suggested (about 15 to 20 minutes on a daily basis), placing primary emphasis on oral expression and a secondary emphasis on transferring that oral expression to written form. If the amount or level of reading involved on the activity pages is inappropriate for a specific class or group, you can modify the lesson by reading the activity page to students and assisting them in recording their responses. Helpful key words may be written on the chalkboard, or students can work in small groups with a good writer serving as the "secretary." On some activity sheets, role playing or drawing a picture is suggested as a mode of expression. This is not intended to penalize students who are not skilled actors or artists, because oral language will be the true focus of all the activities.

The activity pages can be sent home at your discretion. The letters to parents should precede the activity pages so that parents will have some idea of the purpose served by the activities. And don't overlook the very real language opportunity that exists in having your students explain to their parents what a given activity was all about!

Use these activities as they are each day, then expand upon them as you desire. You'll see and hear the results when your students are able to express themselves more clearly and enjoy conversing with others successfully. Best wishes to you and your students!

Darlene Mannix

TABLE OF CONTENTS

Section IV   ACTIVITIES TO HELP STUDENTS WITH THEIR EVERYDAY COMMUNICATION SKILLS   175

SKILLS INDEX

section I

ACTIVITIES TO HELP STUDENTS UNDERSTAND AND RESPOND TO QUESTIONS

1

THE GOALS OF SECTION I ARE

- To improve understanding of, and responses to, "yes/no" questions.
- To improve understanding of and responses to "wh--" (who? what? where? when?) questions.

The first goal is met by offering your students the first 6 activity pages. These sheets are followed by 15 activity pages for understanding who? what? where? and when? questions.

All of the activities can be discussed and responded to orally; however, if you are also concerned about your students' written expression, many of the activities can include elements of writing. You might, for example, have the students write their questions and answers to the activity sheet.

The activities can also be performed in small groups, with students providing oral input and one student acting as the recorder for each small group.

RE: Understanding and responding to questions

Dear Parents,

As part of our oral expression or language time, we are going to be working on *answering questions*. While this might seem like a pretty easy task, it's not! Part of good communication is understanding what information someone wants to know so that you, the answerer of the questions, can tell that person exactly what he or she wants! How many times have you asked questions such as: "What did you do today?" "Nothin'." "Who broke my favorite vase?" "I didn't do it." These responses don't exactly give us much information, do they?

Some of the skills we are going to be practicing at school are: answering yes and no questions correctly; adding explanations (not just saying *yes* or *no*, but telling a bit more); answering questions that ask about who, what, where, when, and how something happens.

There are many ways you can help your child with these skills at home, just by doing day-to-day activities. For example, when you ask your child a yes or no question, don't stop with a simple one-word answer. Have him or her explain why or provide a little more information. (Example: "Did you have fun at school today?" "Yes." "Tell me about it.")

Other examples: When you and your child are doing something together at home such as making cookies, cleaning off the kitchen table, picking up toys, etc., ask him some of the wh_____ questions. "Where did you get this old teddy bear?" "When did you get this?"

It is also good practice for you to pretend you don't know how to do something (making the bed?) and have your child explain the steps to you. Try to follow his directions and see if you end up with a well-made bed!

Many times we, as parents, end up *telling* our children a lot more than *asking* them. Use questions as often as you can with them. See what kind of information comes out!

Sincerely,

_____

Teacher

I-1 THE ANSWER IS "YES"

Objective The student will respond appropriately to questions requiring an affirmative response.

Directions

To the teacher: You may wish to have the class complete the worksheets together if the reading or writing level is low in the class. You may read the question to the students, and have them suggest possible responses for the child on the worksheet.

To the student: You are going to look at four stories. The child in each story needs to answer a question, and you are going to help that child give an answer. The answer to each story is going to start with a "yes."

Answers

The responses may vary somewhat, but typical affirmative responses include:

1. "Yes, I have them right here."
2. "Yes, Mr. Jones, I took it off your desk while you were gone."
3. "Yes, I can see fine from back here."
4. "Yes, Sally is at home in bed with the flu."

THE ANSWER IS "YES"

I-2   THE ANSWER IS "NO"

Objective: The student will respond appropriately to questions requiring a negative response.

Directions

To the teacher: You may want to have the class respond orally to these activities, or work together.

To the student: You are going to look at four stories. The child in each story needs to answer a question, and you are going to help him or her give an answer. The answer to every question is going to start with a "no." See if you can use the picture clues to decide why the child is saying "no."

Answers

The responses may vary somewhat, but typical negative responses include

1. "No, I have my pencil right here."
2. "No, we're going out to the playground."
3. "No, I'm almost finished with this easy page."
4. "No, I'm wearing my glasses."

THE ANSWER IS "NO"

I-3 SHOULD I ANSWER "YES" OR "NO"?

Objective: The student will respond appropriately to questions requiring either an affirmative or a negative response.

Directions

To the teacher: On this sheet, the student is to use picture clues to determine whether the child in the situation would answer "yes" or "no."

To the student: You are going to look at four stories again. Look very carefully at the picture for clues that may help you decide if the child is answering "yes" to the question, or "no."

Answers

Responses may vary, but typical responses include:

1. "No, my daddy is getting me today."
2. "Yes, that is my book." (Note: name on book)
3. "Yes, I ordered chicken today."
4. "No, I ride Bus 30."

NAME _____   DATE _____

SHOULD I ANSWER "YES" OR "NO"?

1.

Is your mother coming to pick you up?

2.

Is this your book, David?

DAVID

3.

Did you order chicken for lunch today, Bob?

4.

Do you ride bus 17?

30

I-4 EITHER "YES" OR "NO"

Objective: The student will respond appropriately to questions requiring either an affirmative or a negative response.

Directions

To the teacher: The question in these situations is presented to two children in each story. One child is going to answer with a "yes," the other is going to answer with a "no." The students should realize that the same question can be answered appropriately either way, depending on the circumstances.

To the student: In these stories, someone is going to ask the same question of two different children. One child is going to answer with a "yes," and the other will answer with a "no." See if you can figure out what each child answered, and what clues helped you.

Answers

Typical responses include:

1. "Yes, I'm done, and here it is!" "No, I forgot it."
2. "Yes, we went to the lake." "No, we went horseback riding."
3. "Yes, I'm finished with it." "No, I'm still reading it."
4. "Yes, it's all cleaned out." "No, I'm working on it."

EITHER "YES" OR "NO"

I-5 I CAN'T MAKE UP MY MIND

Objective: The student will respond appropriately to questions requiring either an affirmative or a negative response.

Directions

To the teacher: On this sheet, someone is asking a question of one individual, but the individual will respond first with a "yes," and then with a "no." The idea is not that the individual really "changes his or her mind," but that the same question could be answered either way by that individual.

To the student: You are going to look at four stories again. This time someone is asking a question of a child. The first time, the child is going to answer the question with a "yes" answer, and the second time the child is going to answer that same question with a "no" answer. There are no picture clues, and no real "right" answer. Let's see if you can answer the question for the child *both* ways.

Answers

Typical responses include:

1. "Yes, I have the paintbrushes." "No, I didn't take them."
2. "Yes, she's here." "No, she's home sick with a cold."
3. "Yes, I saw it on your desk." "No, I haven't seen it."
4. "Yes, I put it there this morning." "No, it's in my desk."

I CAN'T MAKE UP MY MIND

I-6   TELL ME ABOUT YOURSELF

Objective: The student will respond appropriately to questions requiring either an affirmative or a negative response.

Directions

To the teacher: Students can respond orally or in writing, depending on the ability level of the class. If posed orally, the questions should be addressed to specific students, and several students should be allowed to answer the question. Ideally, "Are you sitting down?" for example, should be asked of at least one student who is sitting down and one who is not. Answering completely should be emphasized ("No, I am not sitting down," rather than "No.").

To the student: Today you are going to (read/hear) some questions and decide if you are going to answer with a "yes" answer, or with a "no" answer. Some of the questions may be silly ones, so watch out for them. Write your answer on the line next to the question (optional, if doing orally).

Answers

Depending on the ability level of the students, you may require a full response, or simply a yes/no response to indicate that the student understood the question. Answers will vary.

TELL ME ABOUT YOURSELF

1. Are you a girl? _____

2. Are you a boy? _____

3. Are you a dog? _____

4. Do you have a dog? _____

5. Do you have a cat? _____

6. Do you have an elephant? _____

7. Is your hair black? _____

8. Is your hair green? _____

9. Do you like to eat pizza? _____

10. Do you like to eat leaves? _____

11. Do you have a brother? _____

12. Do you have a sister? _____

13. Do you have legs? _____

14. Do you have a tail? _____

15. Do you know the alphabet? _____

16. Do you have a birthday? _____

17. Do you have two feet? _____

18. Do you have three eyes? _____

19. Do you live in a house? _____

20. Do you live in a bus? _____

21. Do you ride in a car to school? _____

22. Do you walk to school? _____

23. Can you sing? _____

24. Can you fly? _____

25. Can you walk on your hands? _____

I-7 WHO DID IT?

Objective: The student will respond appropriately to "who"/"whose" questions by saying "I" or the name of a person.

Directions

To the teacher: On this worksheet, the student will put a circle around the child in each story who is answering the question appropriately. You may wish to have the student put an X on the child who is not answering appropriately so that he or she will look at both responses carefully.

To the student: You are going to look at five stories. In each story, the teacher is asking a question that begins with the word "who." That means the teacher wants to know the *name* of somebody. One of the children in each story is telling the teacher what the teacher wants to know. The other child is saying something that really doesn't answer the teacher's question. I want you to put a circle around the child who is answering the teacher's question.

Answers

1. first child
2. second child
3. second child
4. second child
5. first child

WHO DID IT?

I-8 WHO? QUESTIONS

Objective: The student will respond appropriately to "who" or "whose" questions by saying "I" or the name of a person.

Directions

To the teacher: On this worksheet, the student is going to look at a classroom of children. Each child on the page can be described in some way. The teacher will describe a child and have the student locate that child by circling him or her or a nearby object. Then the teacher will pose a "who" question and select students to answer the question orally, using a complete response form. You may wish to go over the names of the children on the front of each desk.

To the student: This is a picture of a class of children who are at school. First, I want you to find the child who is reading a book. Now, put a circle around his book. Did you find him? Now, who can answer this question for me: *Who is reading a book? (Answer:* David is reading a book.)

Now I want you to find the child who is raising her arm. I want you to put a circle around her hand as soon as you find her. Got it? Now, who can answer this question for me: *Who is raising her arm? (Answer:* Susan is raising her arm.)

This time I want you to find a child who is holding an apple. Put a circle around the apple. Did you find it? Now, who can answer this question: *Who has an apple? (Answer:* Tony has an apple.)

Now I am going to name a child in the picture, and I want you to try to make up a "who" question about him or her. Ready? Find Jack. What's a good "who" question we could ask about Jack?" (*Answer:* Who is scratching his head?)

Continue this procedure through several of the children in the picture. Students in the class may wish to have other students guess which child they are describing.

Sample Questions

Andy –Who is wearing a striped shirt?

Linda–Who is writing with a pencil?

Tim –Who has on a number shirt?

Patty–Who has pigtails?

WHO? QUESTIONS

I-9 SELECT THE "WHO" ANSWER

Objective: The student will respond appropriately to "who" questions by saying "I" or the name of a person.

Directions

To the teacher: Three possible responses are provided for each of the "who" questions on this page. Only one is the name or description of a person; the other two may be somewhat related, but do not really answer the question. Even though the student may not be familiar with the situation (for example, 1. Who has blue mittens?), by knowing that a *who* question requires a person's name or description as an answer, he should be able to eliminate the inappropriate responses. You may wish to have the students discuss how they knew that the decoy responses could not have been the right answers.

To the student: There are 10 "who" questions on this page. What kind of answer are you going to look for if it's a "who" question? (Allow time for responses.) Listen to/read each question, and see if you can find and circle the *one* correct answer in each row.

Answers

1. Bobby
2. Mary
3. Sally
4. my mother
5. Johnny
6. Superman
7. a boy
8. a little girl
9. a baby
10. I

SELECT THE "WHO" ANSWER

1. Who has blue mittens?   the dog   Bobby   a green tree

2. Who has a pencil?   Mary   the frog   the desk

3. Who has a birthday in October?   cake   party   Sally

4. Who can read a book?   my mother   the library   pages

5. Who has black hair?   Johnny   the book   my teddy bear

6. Who can fly?   a ladder   Superman   the dog

7. Who is 10 years old?   a house   a table   a boy

8. Who has a pet frog?   the pond   green   a little girl

9. Who is crying?   a baby   a pony   sad

10. Who broke the record?   music   the frog   I

I-10 WHAT IS IT?

Objective: The student will respond appropriately to "what" questions that require a specific response by stating that response.

Directions

To the teacher: The student will put a circle around the response in each story that answers the "what" question. In some situations, one child is giving two responses; only one is correct. In other situations, two children are each giving one response; again, only one is correct.

To the student: You are going to look at five stories. In each story, the teacher is asking a child or children a "what" question. That means the teacher wants to know about something. Either one or two children are going to give an answer in the stories, but only one of the answers really tells the teacher what she or he wants to know. The other answer might tell something about the situation, but it doesn't really answer the question. I want you to put a circle around the answer that really tells the teacher what she or he wants to know.

Answers

1. second response
2. first response
3. first response
4. second response
5. second response

WHAT IS IT?

I-11   WHAT? QUESTIONS

Objective: The student will respond appropriately to "what" questions that require a specific response by stating that response.

Directions

To the teacher: The student will look at a picture of a classroom scene. You will describe something in the picture and ask a "what" question that students will answer.

To the student: I am going to talk about some things in the picture. I want you to find the things I am talking about and see if you can tell me the answer to my "what" question.

1. Find the two girls at the table. Something has fallen on the floor next to the girls. I want you to put an X on it. Now, who can answer this question? *What is on the floor by the girls?* (**Answer:** A paintbrush is on the floor.)

2. Look at the chalkboard and find something that is drawn on it. Put an X on it. Can you answer this question? *What is drawn on the chalkboard?* (**Answer:** A house is drawn on the chalkboard.)

3. The teacher put something on top of the chalkboard. Put a circle around it. Can you answer this question? *What is on top of the chalkboard?* (**Answer:** A flag is on top of the chalkboard.)

4. Find the girl who is looking at something in a box. Put a circle around the box. Who can answer this? *What is in the box.* (**Answer:** A kitten is in the box.)

5. The same girl has her foot on something. Put an X on that thing. Now, who can answer this? *What is the girl's foot on?* (**Answer:** The girl's foot is on a book.)

6. Find the two boys. The boy with the dark pants is holding something. Put an X on it. Who can answer this question? *What is the boy holding?* (**Answer:** The boy is holding a bat.)

7. The other boy is holding something, too. Put a circle around it. Who can answer this question? *What is the boy holding?* (**Answer:** The boy is holding a basketball.)

8. One of the boys has something on his head. Put an X on it. Now, who can answer this? *What is on the boy's head?* (**Answer:** The boy has a hat/cap on his head.)

WHAT? QUESTIONS

I-12   SELECT THE "WHAT" ANSWER

Objective: The student will respond appropriately to "what" questions that require a specific response by stating that response.

Directions

To the teacher: Three possible responses are provided for each of the "what" questions on this page. Only one answers the question. Remind the students that a *what* question signals them to look for an answer that is not necessarily a person (that would be a *who* question), but something that fits the description of the word clues given in the question. You may wish to have the students discuss how they arrived at the correct answer by eliminating the incorrect responses.

To the student: There are 10 "what" questions on this page. Remember to look for the answer that fits the description of the thing looked for in the question. Listen to/read each question, and see if you can find and circle the *one* correct answer in each row.

Answers

1. horse
2. house
3. pizza
4. sky
5. duck
6. bird
7. hat
8. elephant
9. a frog ("Steve" would be "who")
10. eating

SELECT THE "WHAT" ANSWER

1. What animal has four legs?   table   chicken   horse

2. What has a door?   window   house   glass

3. What is good to eat?   pizza   restaurant   hungry

4. What is blue?   dog   tree   sky

5. What can fly?   wind   duck   paper

6. What has eyes?   bird   hands   legs

7. What can you wear on your head?   shoes   hat   Bobby

8. What is big?   elephant   ant   mouse

9. What is in the box?   blue   Steve   a frog

10. What are you doing?   eating   a bed   Jennifer

I-13 WHERE? QUESTIONS

Objective: The student will respond appropriately to "where" questions by stating a location.

Directions

To the teacher: The student will locate objects around the room depicted on the worksheet. Students will make up "where" questions about the objects and answer the questions orally. Remind students that a "where" question tells them to answer by telling a place or location of something.

To the student: This is a picture of a classroom. There are objects all over it, and I am going to talk about some of them. See if you can find the things I am talking about. Then I am going to have you make up "where" questions about them and answer them.

1. Can you find the apple in the picture? Put a circle around it. Now, who can ask a "where" question about the apple? (Where is the apple?) Who can answer the question? (The apple is on the chair.)

2. Can you find the ball in the picture? Put a circle around it. Now, who can ask a "where" question about the ball? (Where is the ball?) Who can answer the question? (The ball is under the table.)

3. Can you find the pencil in the picture? Put a circle around it. Now, who can ask a "where" question about the pencil? (Where is the pencil?) Who can answer the question? (The pencil is on the rug/on the floor.)

4. Can you find the book? Put a circle around it. Now, who can ask a "where" question about the book? (Where is the book?) Who can answer the question? (The book is on the table/next to the boy.)

5. Can you find the glass? Put a circle around it. Now, who can ask a "where" question about the glass? (Where is the glass?) Who can answer the question? (The glass is under the chair/on the floor.)

WHERE? QUESTIONS

I-14   WHERE IS IT?

Objective: The student will respond appropriately to "where" questions by stating a location.

Directions

To the teacher: The student will put a circle around the response in each story that answers the "where" question. In each situation, one child is giving two responses; however, only one response answers the question. Remind students that a "where" question signals them to look for a place or location of something.

To the student: You are going to look at five stories. In each story, the first person, a teacher, is asking a "where" question. That means he or she wants to know a *place* where something is. The second person, a student, is giving two answers, but only one of those answers tells where something is. I want you to put a circle around that answer.

Answers

1. second response
2. first response
3. second response
4. second response
5. second response

WHERE IS IT?

1.

Jennifer where is your homework?

What homework?

I left it at home.

2.

Where did you put your lunch money?

I put it on your desk

I had $1.00.

3.

Where is your pencil?

My pencil is yellow.

My pencil is on the art table.

4.

Where did Susan go?

Susan is in trouble.

Susan went to the office.

5.

Where are the markers?

I need the markers!

They are in the art box.

I-15   SELECT THE "WHERE" ANSWER

The student will respond appropriately to "where" questions by stating a location.

Directions

To the teacher: Three possible responses are provided for each of the "where" questions on this page. Only one is the appropriate place or location. Remind the student that a *where* question signals him to look for a place or location.

To the student: There are 10 "where" questions on this page. What kind of answer are you going to look for if it's a "where" question? (allow time for responses) Listen to/read each question, and see if you can find and circle the *one* correct answer in each row. Some of the answers may be almost right, but try to find the one that is the *best* answer.

Answers

1. in a refrigerator
2. in a lake
3. at a zoo
4. in a tree
5. at home
6. by the closet
7. in a garage
8. in front of its house
9. behind the desk
10. on a box

SELECT THE "WHERE" ANSWER

1. Where can you put things to keep them cold?

   in a box   in a refrigerator   in a shoe

2. Where can you go swimming?

   in a lake   in a boat   in a house

3. Where can you see a tiger?

   in a boat   on a dish   at a zoo

4. Where is the bird?

   under the stove   under the hole   in a tree

5. Where is Beth?

   at home   in a shoe   under the zoo

6. Where is the broom?

   in my bookbag   in the tree   by the closet

7. Where is the car?

   in a garage   in a pond   in a zoo

8. Where is the big dog?

   jumping   sleeping   in front of its house

9. Where is my pencil?

   behind the desk   yellow   broken

10. Where did you put the toy car?

   on a box   Michael   green car

I-16   WHEN DID IT HAPPEN?

Objective: The student will respond appropriately to "when" questions by stating a time or an event that indicates a time.

Directions

To the teacher: The student will put a circle around the response in each story that answers the "when" question. In each situation, one child is giving a response that correctly answers the question; the other child is giving a response that may be somewhat related, but does not answer the question. Remind the students to look for words that indicate a *time* or *passage of time* to answer the "when" question.

To the student: You are going to look at five stories. In each story, the teacher is asking a "when" question. That means he or she wants to know a time that tells when something happened or is going to happen. I want you to decide which student is answering the teacher's question and put a circle around that answer.

Answers

1. first child
2. second child
3. second child
4. first child
5. second child

NAME _____   DATE _____

WHEN DID IT HAPPEN?

I-17 WHEN? QUESTIONS

Objective: The student will respond appropriately to "when" questions by stating a time or an event that indicates a time.

Directions

To the teacher: The student will look at four pictures while the teacher reads a short story about the picture. The student will be listening for the words that answer a "when" question about the situation.

To the student: I am going to read you four short stories while you look at a picture about each story. Listen carefully and see if you can answer the "when" question that I will ask you at the end of the story. Listen for words that tell a time or tell *after* or *before* something.

1. Mary's class is going to go to a book sale in the library after they have art. *When will Mary's class go to the book sale?* (**Answer:** after art)
2. David's mother picked him up from school at one o'clock because he had to go to the dentist. *When did David's mother pick him up?* (**Answer:** at one o'clock)
3. Debby and Sandy went to the library on Tuesday. They got some books about horses. *When did they go to the library?* (**Answer:** on Tuesday)
4. Nick and Wally wanted to play softball after school. They got their gloves and went to the field behind the school. *When did they want to play softball?* (**Answer:** after school)

WHEN? QUESTIONS

I-18 SELECT THE "WHEN" ANSWER

Objective: The student will respond appropriately to "when" questions by stating a time or an event that indicates time.

Directions

To the teacher: Three possible responses are given for each of the "when" questions on this page. Only one correctly or appropriately answers the question because it indicates a time or passage of time. The students are to circle the response that could answer the "when" question.

To the student: There are 10 "when" questions on this page. You are going to try to find the one answer that tells when something could happen. Remember that these answers don't necessarily have to be the same as the way things are in our school; you are looking for an answer that would be correct for anybody. Keep in mind that you are looking for words that indicate a time by telling a day, before or after something, or an actual time on a clock. Circle the answer in each row that fits the question.

Answers

1. on Monday
2. 11:30
3. after school
4. after lunch
5. in a few minutes
6. in January
7. tomorrow
8. in two weeks
9. on Fridays
10. in two weeks

SELECT THE "WHEN" ANSWER

1. When do we have art?   on Monday   papier-mâché   painting

2. When do we eat lunch?   cafeteria   11:30   in the lunchroom

3. When do you leave school?   on the bus   at home   after school

4. When do you go out for recess?   if we finish math   1,000   after lunch

5. When will the buses come?   in a few minutes   here   in the parking lot

6. When is the school play?   in the gym   in January   outside

7. When is the basketball game?   tomorrow   in the gym   the captain

8. When will the books come?   in a box   on a bus   in two weeks

9. When do you have music?   on Fridays   singing   with a piano

10. When do we have Christmas vacation?   in a box   in two weeks   yes

I-19   HOW DID IT HAPPEN?

Objective: The student will respond appropriately to "how (did)" questions by giving a reasonable explanation for the event in question.

Directions

To the teacher: The student will put a circle around the response in each story that answers the "how did" question. In each situation, a teacher is asking two students the question. Both students respond, but only one gives an appropriate answer.

To the student: You are going to look at five stories. In each story, a teacher is asking the children how something happened. That means he or she wants to know a reason that caused something to happen, or an explanation. Two children are answering each question, but only one of them is giving an answer that tells a reason. I want you to circle the child who is telling the teacher what the teacher wants to know.

Answers

1. first child
2. first child
3. second child
4. second child
5. second child

HOW DID IT HAPPEN?

I-20   HOW DID? QUESTIONS

Objective: The student will respond appropriately to "how (did)" questions by giving a reasonable explanation for the event in question.

Directions

To the teacher: The student will look at four stories. In each story-picture, a situation is depicted for which the student might ask a "how did (something happen)" question. The student will write or tell what he or she thinks the child in the picture might be asking. When the responses are discussed, students can think of answers to the questions they came up with.

To the student: You are going to look at four pictures. Each picture shows a story about something happening at school. I want you to look at each picture and think about what is happening. What is a "how" question that the child might be asking? Write it in the balloon. (If this activity is done orally, have the students think of a response and raise their hands.) Then we will think of answers to your questions.

Answers

Answers may vary, but typical questions and answers include:

1. How did you get up there? I climbed on the table and the box and then the chair.
2. How do you throw a football? You hold it with your fingers on the laces, like this.
3. How did this dog get in here? Oh, no, I must have left the door at home open again.
4. How did my pencil break? Michael stepped on it when you left it on the floor.

HOW DID? QUESTIONS

I-21 HOW DO YOU DO THAT?

Objective: The student will respond appropriately to "how (do)" questions by giving a reasonable explanation for the event in question.

Directions

To the teacher: The student will answer "how did" questions about some experiences he or she may have had at home or school. The teacher must be sure that the students have had exposure to the activity so that they can describe or explain it. In some cases, the teacher may wish to have the class actually participate in the activity (for example, making popcorn) before questions are asked. The teacher may also wish to add to the list those activities with which the class is familiar and able to explain the various steps involved in performing them. This exercise may best be accomplished by having students select one or two activities they are interested in explaining; then use this as an oral activity.

To the student: I am going to ask you some questions about how to do things. I want you to think about how you would tell another person to do these things so that he or she would understand what you mean. (For students who will be reading the list, the teacher may add: "Take a few minutes to look over the list, and pick out a few items that you would be interested in answering for all of us.")

Answers

Answers will vary, but appropriate responses should include correctly sequencing the steps involved in the activity, labeling the objects used, and being clear or concise with the explanation.

HOW DO YOU DO THAT?

1. How do you play a record?

2. How do you make a paper airplane?

3. How do you make the color *green* with paints?

4. How do you brush your teeth?

5. How do you make lemonade?

6. How do you throw a frisbee?

7. How do you make a hot fudge sundae?

8. How do you make a paper chain?

9. How do you make popcorn?

10. How do you jump rope?

11. How do you wash your hands?

12. How do you sharpen your pencil?

13. How do you make an ice cube melt?

14. How do you braid yarn?

15. How do you play "tag"?

ENRICHMENT ACTIVITIES

TELL ME ABOUT YOURSELF (I-6) can be extended by selecting one child at a time to be highlighted. Other children are allowed to ask that child questions about himself or herself. They may want to know about family, pets, things he or she likes to do, travel, other experiences. Encourage the highlighted child to extend the answer beyond a simple yes or no!

THE SILLY YES/NO GAME is an extension of all of the yes/no activities. The teacher can make a card with YES on one side and NO on the other. When the YES side is displayed, the highlighted child has to answer all questions with a "Yes + extension." When the NO side is displayed, the child must answer the questions with a "No + extension." The teacher may pick one child to control the YES/NO card (flipping it back and forth after every few questions). Two other children are picked as the questioners. They can ask the highlighted child (or children, as this can be played with several children picked to respond) silly questions, remembering that the fun of the answer will depend on whether the card is on the YES or NO side. For example, questions might be: "Do you have purple hair?" and if the YES side is displayed, the child must answer: "Yes, I have purple hair." If the question posed was: "Do you want to eat pizza?" the child may answer, "No, I don't want to eat pizza." Children can take turns holding the card, answering and asking questions.

WHO? QUESTIONS (I-8) and *WHAT? QUESTIONS (I-11)* can be extended by using the real classroom situation to ask and answer questions. The teacher may wish to look around the room and pose such questions as: Who has a blue shirt on today? Who is not sitting up? What is on the window sill? What is the new toy on the playground? In this manner, the children's attention will be directed to real-life situations, rather than simulations on worksheets.

WHERE IS IT? (I-14) can be extended by playing a variation of the game Simon Says. The teacher or model places her hands at a certain location, for example, on her head. She will then instruct the children: "Do this." The children will have to model her by placing their hands on their heads. Then ask the children, "Where are your hands?" and they respond, "On my head." By saying, "Do this," instead of "Put your hands under the table" the children have to *look* as well as listen, and then think about their answer instead of simply imitating. Keep the pace FAST! Once the students understand the game, student leaders can direct it.

TREASURE HUNT is another game that extends WHERE IS IT? (I-14). The teacher (at first—later, students) hides something in the room while several students are outside. The incoming students must ask questions of the students who know where the object or "treasure" is hidden. They will not actually be asking "where" questions, but will be using location words. "Is it under the shelf?" "Is it next to the red book?" "Is it on the back table?" The teacher then responds, "No, that's not *where* it is."

BEFORE AND AFTER is an activity that builds upon WHEN? QUESTIONS (I-17). Activities that routinely take place in school during the day can be discussed in sequential order and listed on the board. Questions of a "before and after" nature can then be asked. "When do we have art? Is it before gym or after recess? After math or before spelling?" Events can also be sequenced according to clock time, with the time written next to them. The child may then learn that art (e.g., which comes at 9:30) is right *before* recess (e.g., which comes at 10:15). The teacher can direct numerous questions using this list, for example, "When do we have music?" could be answered by "Monday, 2:30, before science, *or* after health." All would be correct!

A DAY IN MY LIFE is an extension activity of "when" concepts. Each child can draw the activities that are part of his or her day. It may begin with getting up, brushing teeth, riding the bus to school, and continue through school activities, on into what happens in the evening. Each activity should be drawn on a separate piece of paper. Activity pages can then be sequenced according to what he or she does during the day. The children can compile their sheets into a book and share their day with one another.
     An alternative way to do this is to fold one sheet of paper into fourths and use each of the four panels to depict one event in the day. Be sure the student numbers them 1-2-3-4!

HOW DID IT HAPPEN (I-19) can be done with pictures, either taken from magazines, newspapers, photographs, or child-generated drawings. This can be a creative writing/talking experience for the child to explain how something in the picture happened. Some (for example, a broken window) may be pretty obvious at first, but children can be encouraged to embellish their stories. They don't have to be 100 percent factual, just fun! Make sure the pictures selected depict an *event—*something has to have happened!

TALENT SHOW is similar to HOW DO YOU DO THAT? (I-21). Children who really are talented at something can perform for the rest of the class and be prepared to field questions the rest of the students may want to ask. Who knows—maybe you have some budding juggler or fantastic future chef sitting in Row 3!

SHOW AND ANSWER is similar to Show and Tell, except the highlighted child cannot tell; he or she can only *answer* questions that the other students ask. Another rule that has worked well is that every child *has* to ask a question. It may be helpful at first to restrict this game to having objects brought in, rather than events related. The highlighted child displays the object and waits for the questions. You'll find that children ask questions they are really interested in finding the answers to. No doubt you'll hear things like "Can it go backward?" or "What would happen if you pulled all its legs off?" Curious children ask questions! Let's hope your students will be able to answer them appropriately!

section II

ACTIVITIES TO HELP STUDENTS IMPROVE THEIR PROBLEM-SOLVING ABILITIES

THE GOAL OF SECTION II IS

- To improve problem-solving abilities by expressing logical and reasonable answers to questions.

This section focuses on using verbal skills to assist in solving problems in classroom situations. In particular, the activities require the student to identify a problem, devise logical or reasonable solutions, and express these ideas to others.

Section II contains 29 activity sheets, using a variety of response modes. On some, a multiple-choice format is used, in which the student must determine the most appropriate response. Others involve having the student draw a picture that depicts what he or she thinks the character with the problem could do. It is not of particular importance that the drawings be detailed or even recognizable, as the prime objective is for the student to express his or her ideas verbally. As an alternative, students could explain or write their responses on the activity sheets.

Re: Improving problem-solving abilities

Dear Parents,

For the next few weeks, our class will be learning about ways to solve problems—in particular, how to give logical and reasonable answers to questions.

The first skill area we'll be working on is answering *"why"* questions with a logical explanation. Throughout the day at home, you can take advantage of opportunities to ask your child questions such as the following: "Why do you have to wear mittens today? Why do we use a spoon to eat soup? Why do you have to brush your teeth? Why should you be quiet while the baby is taking a nap?"

Other problem-solving skills involve *predicting* what will happen next. You might ask questions like, "That dog looks pretty muddy to me...guess what I'm going to do with her?" or "This car is almost out of gas. What do you think our next errand is going to be?" or "These potato chips are not our usual brand, but they are on sale this week. Which do you think I'm going to buy? Why?"

Sequencing—or listing the steps you need to do in the order you need to do them—is another area we'll be working on. You can use lots of questions to help your child figure out the steps involved in everyday activities. For example, "What do we do *first* to get ready for a bath? *Then* what? And *after* that? What do we do at the *end*?"

Look for situations throughout the day that can be helpful in introducing problem solving to your child at home. We'll be doing the same thing at school!

Sincerely,

_____

Teacher

II-1 TELL ME WHY

Objective: The student will answer "why" questions appropriately by stating a logical explanation for an event.

Directions

To the teacher: The student will examine a picture while the teacher asks a "why" question about characters in the picture. Three possible explanations are given; the student must select the most plausible reason. The student is to put an X in the box preceding the response selected. You may wish to read all three responses to the students and discuss why each is or is not a logical answer.

To the student: While you are looking at each picture, I am going to ask you a question about someone in the picture. I want you to think about *why* that person is doing what he is doing. There are three answers on the side that give reasons for why the person is doing something; I want you to pick out the best answer and put an X in that box.

1. Why is Sally wearing a coat? (**Answer:** b)
2. Why should you put your name on your paper? (**Answer:** c)
3. Why should the class be quiet while the teacher is giving a lesson? (**Answer:** a)

NAME _____   DATE _____

II-1

TELL ME WHY

1.

☐ a. it is dark out

☐ b. to keep warm

☐ c. she forgot her sweater

2.

☐ a. so you will remember your name

☐ b. so you can use your new pencil

☐ c. so you and your teacher will know which paper is yours

3.

☐ a. so everyone can hear the teacher

☐ b. so everyone can hear you

☐ c. so you can see the teacher

II-2 WHAT IS THE REASON?

Objective: The student will answer "why" questions appropriately by stating a logical explanation for an event.

Directions

To the teacher: The procedure is similar to that of II-1; the student is to put an X in front of the answer that best tells why a character in the picture is doing something. Discuss why each response is or is not appropriate.

To the student: I am going to ask you a question about each picture—why a character is doing something or what he or she should do. There are three answers on the side that give reasons why that person is doing something. I want you to pick out the best answer and put an X in that box.

1. Why should you wash your hands before you go to lunch? (**Answer:** c)
2. Why should you sharpen your pencil before class starts? (**Answer:** a)
3. Why should you put the top on the paste jar when you're finished with it? (**Answer:** c)

NAME _____   DATE _____

II-2

WHAT IS THE REASON?

1.

☐ a. so your hands will be wet when you touch your food

☐ b. so your hands will be warm when you touch your food

☐ c. so your hands will be clean when you touch your food

2.

☐ a. so you will be ready to do your work

☐ b. so you can make noise

☐ c. so you can walk around

3.

☐ a. so you will know where the paste is

☐ b. so you will know where the paper is

☐ c. so the paste won't dry up

II-3 DO YOU KNOW WHY?

Objective: The student will answer "why" questions appropriately by stating a logical explanation for an event.

Directions

To the teacher: The student is to put an X in front of the answer that best tells why a character in the picture is doing something. Discuss why each response is or is not appropriate.

To the student: I am going to ask you a question about each picture—why a character is doing something or should do something. There are three answers on the side that give reasons; I want you to pick the best answer and put an X in that box.

1. Why should Tommy pick up his books and other things from the floor before he goes home from school? (**Answer:** a)
2. Why should the class walk during a fire drill? (**Answer:** c)
3. Why should you be ready to go when they call to load the buses? (**Answer:** c)

DO YOU KNOW WHY?

1.

☐ a. so he can find his things later

☐ b. so he can play on the floor

☐ c. so he won't forget where he sits

2.

☐ a. so the class can see the fire

☐ b. so the class will be the last one outside

☐ c. so the teacher can easily see the class

3.

☐ a. so you can run down the hall

☐ b. so you can sleep on the bus

☐ c. so you won't miss your bus

II-4 WHAT MIGHT HAPPEN?

Objective: The student will supply at least two appropriate responses when asked to predict what might happen with events that have several possible outcomes.

Directions

To the teacher: The student will be presented with pictures showing children in problem situations. Each student will be asked to draw a picture showing what might happen next—either what the child in the situation might choose to do or what a next logical event might be. After completing their drawings, students should share their ideas verbally. Conclude the activity by asking students to tell at least two predicted outcomes for the same event. Remember that the drawing serves as *a means* to express ideas, not the end.

To the student: You are going to look at pictures of children at school. I want you to draw a picture of what you think might happen next. There are lots of things that might happen, not just one thing. Try to think of different ideas. Don't worry if you can't draw exactly what you want—you can explain to us what's happening in your picture.

1. What might happen if you forgot your pencil at home?
2. What might happen if the watercolors dried up and you wanted to paint?
3. What might happen if you came to school with chickenpox?

Answers

Suggested responses include:

1. You could borrow one, look in your bookbag, buy one at the bookstore.
2. You could put water in the paints, use another paint set, use poster paint instead.
3. The teacher could call your parent, you could go to the school nurse, you could put your head down, you could have your temperature taken.

NAME _____   DATE _____

WHAT MIGHT HAPPEN?

1.

2.

3.

II-5   WHAT COULD THIS LEAD TO?

Objective: The student will supply at least two appropriate responses when asked to predict what might happen with events that have several possible outcomes.

Directions

To the teacher: As on the previous worksheet, the student will draw a picture showing what might happen next. Students should share their drawings and/or ideas verbally with the class. Conclude the activity by asking students to tell at least two predicted outcomes for the same event.

To the student: You are going to look at pictures of children at school. I want you to draw a picture of what you think might happen next. Remember, there might be lots of different things that could happen. After you're all through, we'll talk about our pictures.

1. What might happen if you broke a shoelace on the playground?
2. What might happen if you forgot your glasses?
3. What might happen if it became very hot in the room?

Answers

Suggested responses include:

1. Tie it back together, tell the teacher, play anyway.
2. Call your parent to bring them, sit closer to the board, have a friend read the problems to you.
3. The teacher might turn on a fan, open the windows, take the class outside.

WHAT COULD THIS LEAD TO?

1.

2.

3.

II-6   WHAT COULD YOU DO?

Objective: The student will supply at least two appropriate responses when asked to predict what might happen with events that have several possible outcomes.

Directions

To the teacher: Students will draw a picture of the next thing that might happen in three different situations. Students should be able to tell at least two predicted outcomes for the same event.

To the student: I want you to draw a picture of what you think might happen next in each of these situations. Then we'll talk about the different ideas you all had.

1. What might happen if it were library day and you couldn't remember what you did with your book?
2. What might happen if someone accidentally knocked over a glass of milk at the lunch table?
3. What might happen if you hurt your leg outside during recess?

Answers

Suggested responses include:

1. You could look in your desk, ask your mom to look at home, look around the room.
2. Your food would get wet, your clothes would get wet, you could get a cloth to wipe it up.
3. You might sit down for awhile, you might tell the teacher, you might get a bandage for it.

WHAT COULD YOU DO?

1.

2.

3.

II-7 THE NEXT EVENT

Objective: The student will respond appropriately when presented with events that have only one probable outcome.

Directions

To the teacher: The student will look at pictures depicting an event. There will be several choices as to what the next event (or object representing the outcome of that event) will be. The student is to circle the appropriate response. The class may benefit from discussing how they arrived at the appropriate answer by eliminating other responses.

To the student: You are going to look at four pictures. I am going to tell you about what's happening in the picture. Then I want you to put a circle around the picture that shows what will happen next. Think about why you picked that answer and we'll talk about it.

1. Tommy was outside on the playground when it began to rain. Tommy thought, "I need to run back in the classroom and get something that I brought to school this morning." What did Tommy get? (**Answer:** umbrella)

2. Kris brought a big box into the classroom. She said, "Look what my sister gave me for my birthday." The other children looked inside and said, "Oh! Can we have one? They look delicious." What was in the box? (**Answer:** cookies)

3. The class had a plant in the room. No one remembered to take care of the plant while they were on vacation from school for two weeks at Christmas. What do you think the plant looked like when the class came back? (**Answer:** the third plant)

4. Alice and Mary were sitting at a table in school. They had finished all their work and wanted to get something to read. "I have something in my desk," said Alice. "I got it at the library." What did Alice get? (**Answer:** book)

THE NEXT EVENT

1.

2.

3.

4.

II-8 THE NEXT THING TO HAPPEN

Objective: The student will respond appropriately when presented with events that have only one probable outcome.

Directions

To the teacher: The student will look at four pictures and listen to a brief description of the event portrayed. He or she will then put an X in the box in front of the sentence that tells what the next event will probably be. Discuss why that response is the most probable outcome.

To the student: You are going to look at four pictures. I am going to tell you about what is happening in the picture. Then I want you to put an X in front of the sentence below each picture which tells what you think will probably happen next.

1. Mike was waiting outside the school for his bus to come. Mike rides Bus 88. A bus pulled up to the school. It had 78 on the side of it. What will probably happen next? (**Answer:** a)

2. Kay was watching the clock and waiting for the 3:00 bell to ring. Her father was going to come to pick her up right after school to take her to the circus. The bell rang. "Oh, good," said Kay. "School's over." What will probably happen next? (**Answer:** b)

3. The teacher told the class that if they played nicely outside during recess, they could have an extra 15 minutes to play. The class played very, very nicely. What probably happened next? (**Answer:** b)

4. In Matt's class, if the children finish all their work at school they don't have to take any homework home. Matt was daydreaming during study time and didn't finish all his reading. What probably happened next? (**Answer:** c)

THE NEXT THING TO HAPPEN

1.

☐ a. Mike will wait for Bus 88.
☐ b. Mike will get on the bus.
☐ c. Mike will get on Bus 30.

2.

☐ a. The circus will start.
☐ b. Kay's father will come.
☐ c. The clock will stop.

3.

☐ a. The class will not have extra recess.
☐ b. The class will have extra recess.
☐ c. The teacher will be angry.

4.

☐ a. Matt will have to finish his spelling.
☐ b. Matt will not have homework.
☐ c. Matt will have homework.

II-9 SEQUENCING EVENTS

Objective: The student will state completely and appropriately the various steps involved in sequencing tasks presented.

Directions

To the teacher: The student will see pictures of two different tasks that show aspects of the task, but are not necessarily in sequence. The student is to number the pictures (1,2,3) in correct sequence. After completing the worksheet, the class can work together to add steps involved in the task and should work on orally stating at least three steps for each task in correct order. Make sure your students have had experience with these tasks before the activity is presented. The activity sheet's pictures can be cut apart to aid in sequencing.

To the student: You are going to see children in pictures doing something you might do sometime. The first pictures are about getting ready for school, but they are not in the right order. What's happening in the first picture? (allow time for discussion) What's happening in the second picture? What about the third picture? Let's see if you can put the pictures in the right order by putting a "1" in the box of the picture that would happen first. Then put a "2" in the box that shows what would happen next. Put a "3" in the box that shows what would happen last. You will do the same for the bottom pictures, which are about getting to school. When we're all finished, I am going to write all of the steps on the board and see if we can add others.

Answers

1. Getting ready for school: 2-3-1
2. Getting to school: 1-3-2

68

SEQUENCING EVENTS

Getting ready for school

Getting to school

II-10   PUTTING EVENTS IN ORDER

Objective: The student will state completely and appropriately the various steps involved in sequencing tasks presented.

Directions

To the teacher: The student will sequence three pictures of an event by placing 1, 2, or 3 in the box by each picture. Make sure your students have had experience with these tasks before presenting this activity. Discuss what's happening in each picture before the students attempt to number them. The activity sheet's pictures can be cut apart for help in sequencing.

To the student: This time we're going to look at pictures of students eating lunch at school and making popcorn. The pictures of these events are not in the right order. We're going to talk about what's happening in each of the pictures and then try to put them in the right order. I want you to put a number "1" in the box by what would happen first. Then put a "2" in the box by what would happen next. And, put a "3" in the box by the picture that shows what would happen last. When we're all finished, we'll list the steps on the board and try to add more.

Answers

1. Eating lunch at school: 2-1-3
2. Making popcorn: 3-2-1

PUTTING EVENTS IN ORDER

II-11 FIRST THIS, THEN THAT

Objective: The student will state completely and appropriately the various steps involved in sequencing tasks presented.

Directions

To the teacher: The student will sequence three pictures of students watering plants and cleaning the chalkboard. Discuss what is happening in each picture before the students sequence the pictures by numbering them 1, 2, or 3. Make sure your students have had experience with these tasks before the activity is presented. The activity sheet's pictures can be cut apart to aid in sequencing.

To the student: On this sheet, you will see mixed-up pictures of children watering plants and cleaning the chalkboard. We're going to talk about what's happening in each picture and see if we can put them in the right order by numbering them 1, 2, and 3 in the little boxes. When we're finished, we'll list the steps on the board and see if we can add more.

Answers

   1. Watering plants: 1-3-2
   2. Cleaning the chalkboard: 1-2-3

FIRST THIS, THEN THAT

Re: Solving problems from different perspectives

Dear Parents,

The next set of problem-solving skills that we'll be working on includes looking at problems and how to solve them from different perspectives—looking for missing information, suggesting many causes and solutions for problems, finding something good and bad about a situation, and viewing a situation by pretending to be something or someone else.

At home, you can playfully make situations for your child so that he or she has to tell you some *missing information*. For example, hand him his plate without food on it, give her the toothbrush without toothpaste, or pretend to send him out the door in winter without his shoes. "Oh, did I forget to do something?" works well. Another idea is to retell a favorite story, but leave something out (like the baby bear in "Goldilocks and the Three Bears").

Another problem-solving skill is that of finding more than one explanation for something happening. At home, use opportunities when your child mentions an interesting event (a burned house, a wrecked car, a splotch of mud on the carpet) and ask him or her what could have caused it. Then ask your child to think about *what else* could have caused it.

Somewhat like that is the skill of finding *many solutions* to problems. This starts the very-adult-process of coming up with many possible ideas, thinking about which ones won't work, and ending up with a thoughtful decision. When your child says, "The wheel fell off my toy car. What should we do?", instead of telling him or her to throw it out right away, you might help list several ideas. "Can we glue it back on? Will the wheel stay on with a pin? Is it worth the trouble to fix it?" Your child can then come to a decision about what to do and follow through with the choice.

Finding something *good and bad* in the same situation is another skill that can be challenging and broadening. Discuss with your child the good or positive aspects of things that might seem only bad (cleaning up her room, rainy Saturdays), and the drawbacks of things that seem only good (getting a new puppy, spending all of his money at one time). This may take some thinking!

Finally, the game of having your child *pretend to be someone or something else* and answer questions as though he or she were that thing is another way to have your child practice taking on another's viewpoint or seeing the world differently. You might ask your child what animal or person he would like to turn into for a day and what he would do during the day. Would your child be able to sit at her classroom desk with big kangaroo feet? Would it be fun to be Santa on Christmas Eve, or would it be hard work? (This activity can best be done while talking late at night with cookies and milk in hand!) Encourage creativity!

In general, encourage your child to look at problems that may be encountered during the day as situations that have lots of causes and lots of answers—it's just a matter of thinking it through and picking the best one to try first!

Sincerely,

_____

Teacher

II-12 MISSING INFORMATION

Objective: The student will provide missing piece(s) of information when an activity is described in which one or more pieces of information essential to completing the activity are omitted.

Directions

To the teacher: The student will look at the pictures while you present the situation in which someone is requesting the child in the picture to do something; however, a piece of information is missing. The student is to ask a question that the child in the picture might ask to obtain the information needed.

To the student: You are going to look at four pictures of children at school. The child in each picture wants to do or know something, but he or she first needs to find out something that's missing. I want you to listen to each story and then think of a question that the child in the picture might ask to find out what he or she needs to know.

1. Mrs. Davis asked Brad if he would deliver a note. Brad said "yes." What else does Brad need to know? What question could he ask? (**Answer:** where the note goes—"Where does this note go?")

2. Angie went to the school store to buy a pencil. She had two dimes in her pocket. There were no prices marked on the pencils, and Angie didn't know if she had enough money to buy one or two. What does she need to know? What question could she ask? (**Answer:** how much the pencils cost—"How much are the pencils?")

3. Ricky went to the cafeteria to eat lunch. He was really hungry and couldn't wait to eat. He hoped that pizza would be served today, but he couldn't see over the counter. What does Ricky need to know? What question could he ask? (**Answer:** what's for lunch— "What are you serving for lunch today?")

4. David's teacher told the class to open their reading books to the next story. David had been absent for a few days and missed reading class. He opened his book, but realized he needed to know something. What does he need to know? What question could he ask? (**Answer:** what's the next story— "What story will we be reading?")

MISSING INFORMATION

1.

2.

3.

4.

II-13 SOMETHING'S MISSING

Objective: The student will provide missing piece(s) of information when an activity is described in which one or more pieces of information essential to completing the activity are omitted.

Directions

To the teacher: The student will examine four pictures while listening to a story in which the child in the picture is asked to do something. The student is to determine what information is missing and ask a question that the child in the picture might ask to obtain that information.

To the student: You are going to look at four pictures of children at school. Each child wants to do or know something, but he or she has to first ask a question to find out some missing information. I want you to listen to each story and then think of a question the child might ask to find out what he or she needs to know.

1. Denise's class was going to go outside to play a new game. Her teacher asked her to go into the closet and get the ball. What does Denise need to know? What question could she ask? (**Answer:** which ball to get—"Which ball should I get?")

2. Carl's teacher told him to go over to her desk and get her something to write with. What does Carl need to know? What question could he ask? (**Answer:** pen or pencil—"Do you want the pen or the pencil?")

3. Mrs. Makit, the art teacher, came into the class. She said, "Today we're going to make Christmas gifts for your parents. Let's get your things ready." What does the class need to know? What question could they ask? (**Answer:** what materials they'll need—"What do we need for today?")

4. Mrs. Dailey turned on the television set, but it was the wrong channel. "Sam," said Mrs. Dailey, "the program we want to watch is not on Channel 9. Could you please change the channel?" What else does Sam need to know? What question could he ask? (**Answer:** what channel she wants—"What channel should I change it to?")

SOMETHING'S MISSING

1.

2.

3.

4.

II-14 MAKING INFERENCES

Objective: The student will make an appropriate inference when a situation is presented.

Directions

To the teacher: The student will look at a picture of a situation while you read a short story in which something is described, but not named or pictured. The student will decide what the inference is and place an X in front of the answer (a, b, or c) on the worksheet. Discuss why that answer is appropriate and the others are not.

To the student: I am going to read some stories to you while you look at a picture that shows what is happening. The children in each story are doing something or looking at something, but I am not going to tell you exactly what it is. Listen for clues and see if you can figure out the answer. Put an X in front of the answer in the box.

1. Kim and Kara went over to the window. "Look," said Kim. "Do you see what I see?" Kara looked. "I see something black. Does he belong to you?" "No," said Kim. "It lives next door to us." What are Kim and Kara looking at? (**Answer:** b)

2. Jim looked at the board, but he could not see what was written on it. He pulled out his bookbag from under his desk and looked for something. "Oh, no," said Jim. "I won't be able to see all day." Why can't Jim see the board? (**Answer:** c)

3. Christopher and his class walked quietly down the hall and turned into a room. They sat at the tables and waited for Miss Pepper to come into the room. "Good afternoon," Miss Pepper said. "Please put your books on my desk so you can get new ones this week." Where are Christopher and his class? (**Answer:** a)

4. Jill was drawing a picture of her house. She was making it bright red like the bricks on the front of her house. She pressed a bit too hard and something broke. "Oh, no," said Jill. "Now I can't finish my picture." What broke? (**Answer:** c)

MAKING INFERENCES

1.

☐ a. A car.
☐ b. A cat.
☐ c. A book.

2.

☐ a. Someone is in front of him.
☐ b. His eyes hurt.
☐ c. He forgot his glasses.

3.

☐ a. At the library.
☐ b. In the gym.
☐ c. In the office.

4.

☐ a. Her paper.
☐ b. Her finger.
☐ c. Her crayon.

II-15   WHAT IS INFERRED?

Objective: The student will make an appropriate inference when a situation is presented.

Directions

To the teacher: The student will look at pictures of situations while the teacher reads a short story in which something is described, but not named or pictured. The student will decide which of three answers best describes the inference suggested. Discuss why that answer is appropriate and the others are not.

To the student: I am going to read some stories to you while you look at a picture that shows what is happening. The children are doing or talking about something, but I am not going to tell you exactly what. Listen for clues and see if you can figure out the answer. Put an X in front of the best answer.

1. It was a very cold afternoon. Michael looked carefully in his bookbag before getting ready to walk home. Something was missing. "Oh, dear," he thought. "My hand is really going to be cold." What was missing? **(Answer:** c)

2. Barbara and Ellen took something out of the closet before they went outside for recess. "Here—catch this," called Barbara as she threw something to Ellen. Ellen wasn't looking, though, and it rolled away. What were the girls playing with? **(Answer:** b)

3. Debby said good-bye to her teacher as she walked toward the door. "I'll see you tomorrow, Mrs. Graham," she called. "Good-bye, Debby," said Mrs. Graham. "I hope you don't have any cavities." Where is Debby going? **(Answer:** c)

4. Philip was the first one in line. He walked up three steps and sat down. "I can't wait to get home," he thought. "I want to tell Mom about what happened in school today." He looked out of the window and waved to his friends. Where is Philip? **(Answer:** b)

WHAT IS INFERRED?

1.

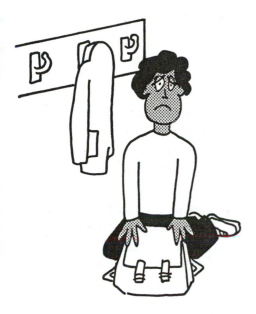

☐ a. A hat.
☐ b. A book.
☐ c. A mitten.

2.

☐ a. A jumprope.
☐ b. A ball.
☐ c. A record.

3.

☐ a. Home.
☐ b. To the park.
☐ c. To the dentist.

4.

☐ a. In the classroom.
☐ b. On the bus.
☐ c. At home.

II-16   WHAT CAN YOU INFER?

Objective: The student will make an appropriate inference when a situation is presented.

Directions

To the teacher: The student will look at pictures of situations while the teacher reads a short story in which something is described, but not named or pictured. The student will decide which of three answers best describes the inference for each situation. Discuss why that answer is appropriate and the others are not.

To the student: I am going to read some stories to you while you look at a picture that shows what is happening. The children are doing something, or they need something, but I won't tell you exactly what. Listen carefully and see if you can figure out what I'm talking about. Then put an X in front of the answer that tells what it is.

1. Valerie looked up and waved. "What are you doing here?" she asked. "You forgot your lunch money," said the person. "I'll see you at home." Who was Valerie talking to? **(Answer:** a)

2. Marlon was doing his math when he went too fast and made a mistake. "I'll have to change that answer," he thought. Then he stopped. "I can't change it with this pencil," he thought. What does Marlon need? **(Answer:** a)

3. David and Skip were playing on the playground when David fell and hurt his foot. "I need to go get something," said David. "I want to cover that scratch before it gets dirt in it." What does David want to get? **(Answer:** b)

4. Jackie and Lisa were sharing something from a bag. "This is so good," said Jackie. "It's really salty." Lisa said, "I know. I like it best with lots of butter on it." What were Jackie and Lisa eating? **(Answer:** a)

NAME _____   DATE _____

WHAT CAN YOU INFER?

1.

☐ a. Her sister.
☐ b. Her teacher.
☐ c. Her dog.

2.

☐ a. An eraser.
☐ b. A piece of paper.
☐ c. A book.

3.

☐ a. A ball.
☐ b. A bandage.
☐ c. A piece of paper.

4.

☐ a. Popcorn.
☐ b. Potato chips.
☐ c. Candy.

II-17 MANY CAUSES

Objective: The student will identify more than one possible cause of an event presented.

Directions

To the teacher: The student will look at pictures depicting an event. There are several reasons that may account for the event. The student will draw (or verbally explain) one possible cause for the event. The class as a whole should orally discuss and compare their drawings or responses to come up with several explanations for the event. At the conclusion of the activity, the student should be able to identify at least two possible causes for each event.

To the student: You are going to look at some pictures that show something happening. First we are going to talk about what is happening in the picture. Then I want you to draw a picture that shows what made the first picture happen. When we are all finished, we are going to share our ideas. Remember, there are lots of reasons why things happen, not just one reason.

Situations and Suggested Responses

1. Music is coming from a classroom.
   - Children singing.
   - Radio or TV on.
   - Tape recorded music.
   - Record player.

2. A school bus is pulling up in front of the school.
   - Time to go home/or arrive at school.
   - Field trip.
   - Moving the bus to parking lot.
   - Time to get gas for the bus.

3. A boy has a broken kite.
   - The kite got caught in a tree.
   - The boy fell and broke the kite.
   - Wind damaged the kite.
   - A dog played with the kite.

MANY CAUSES

1.

2.

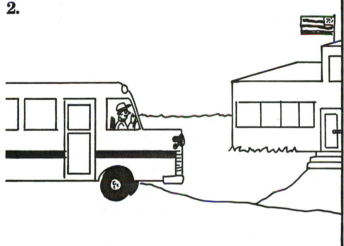

3.

II-18   MANY POSSIBILITIES

Objective: The student will identify more than one possible cause of an event presented.

Directions

To the teacher: The student will look at pictures depicting an event and think of several reasons or explanations for that event. He will then draw (or verbally provide) one possible explanation. The class as a whole should orally discuss and compare their responses. At the conclusion of the activity, the student should be able to identify at least two possible causes for each event.

To the student: You are going to look at pictures that show something happening. We'll talk about what is happening in the picture, and then I want you to draw a picture that explains what made the first picture happen. When we are all finished, we are going to share our ideas.

Situations and Suggested Responses

1. Children are sitting at a table, laughing and smiling.
   - They are listening to the teacher read a funny story.
   - They are watching a funny show on TV.
   - They all got an A on a test.
   - Someone told a joke.

2. A glass of milk has spilled.
   - Someone knocked it over.
   - The wind blew it over.
   - Someone bumped into the table it was on.

3. A boy is walking down the hall with mud on his shirt.
   - He fell down on the way to school.
   - His dog jumped up on him with dirty paws.
   - He was fighting outside and fell down.

MANY POSSIBILITIES

1.

2.

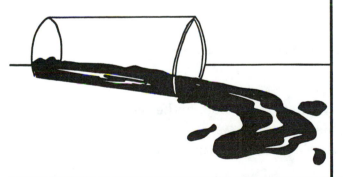

3.

II-19 PROVIDING SOLUTIONS (1)

Objective: The student will identify and explain the problem and provide an appropriate solution when presented with a problem situation.

Directions

To the teacher: The student will be presented with a problem. He or she will first identify the problem (written on the picture), and draw a picture that shows how the child on the worksheet could solve the problem. Problems should then be discussed with the entire class, and suggestions from students shared and considered. Ability to draw is not important; the students can describe their drawings or give a verbal answer.

To the student: You are going to see pictures of children in a class who are having some sort of problem. I want you to think about how each child could solve the problem and draw a picture of what he or she might do. Don't worry if you can't draw very well, because we will be sharing our pictures and our ideas, and you can tell us about your picture. There might be lots of ways each child could get out of the problem, so think about different things that child could do.

Answers

Answers will vary, although some common solutions may include:
- asking the teacher for help
- asking a friend for help
- replacing a missing object by buying or borrowing another one
- making a phone call to mom or dad
- finding something else to do until the problem situation changes

PROVIDING SOLUTIONS (1)

Problem	A solution
John can't get his coat off.	
Mary can't find her pencil.	
Susan can't see the chalkboard.	
Mark forgot his homework.	

II-20 PROVIDING SOLUTIONS (2)

Objective: The student will identify and explain the problem and provide an appropriate solution when presented with a problem situation.

Directions

To the teacher: The student will be presented with a problem. He or she will first identify the problem (written on the picture), and draw a picture that shows how the child on the worksheet could solve the problem. Problems should then be discussed with the entire class, and suggestions from students shared and considered. Ability to draw is not important; the students can describe their drawings or give a verbal answer.

To the student: You are going to see pictures of children in a class who are having some sort of problem. I want you to think about how each child could solve the problem and draw a picture of what he or she might do. Don't worry if you can't draw very well, because we will be sharing our pictures and our ideas, and you can tell us about your picture. There might be lots of ways each child could get out of the problem, so think about different things that child could do.

Answers

Answers will vary, although some common solutions may include:
- asking the teacher for help
- asking a friend for help
- replacing a missing object by buying or borrowing another one
- making a phone call to mom or dad
- finding something else to do until the problem situation changes

PROVIDING SOLUTIONS (2)

Problem	A solution
Andy ripped a page in his reading book.	
Beth ran out of room on her paper.	
Ben's pen ran out of ink.	
David can't reach the pencil sharpener.	

II-21 PROVIDING SOLUTIONS (3)

Objective: The student will identify and explain the problem and provide an appropriate solution when presented with a problem situation.

Directions

To the teacher: The student will be presented with a problem. He or she will first identify the problem (written on the picture), and draw a picture that shows how the child on the worksheet could solve the problem. Problems should then be discussed with the entire class, and suggestions from students shared and considered. Ability to draw is not important; the students can describe their drawings or give a verbal answer.

To the student: You are going to see pictures of children in a class who are having some sort of problem. I want you to think about how each child could solve the problem and draw a picture of what he or she might do. Don't worry if you can't draw very well, because we will be sharing our pictures and our ideas, and you can tell us about your picture. There might be lots of ways each child could get out of the problem, so think about different things that child could do.

Answers

Answers will vary, although some common solutions may include:
- asking the teacher for help
- asking a friend for help
- replacing a missing object by buying or borrowing another one
- making a phone call to mom or dad
- finding something else to do until the problem situation changes

PROVIDING SOLUTIONS (3)

Problem	A solution
Nick is missing a piece of his puzzle. 	
Jennifer forgot what the teacher told her to do. 	
Scott erased so hard that his paper ripped. 	
Alan's nose started to bleed. 	

II-22   PROVIDING SOLUTIONS (4)

Objective: The student will identify and explain the problem and provide an appropriate solution when presented with a problem situation.

Directions

To the teacher: The student will be presented with a problem. He or she will first identify the problem (written on the picture), and draw a picture that shows how the child on the worksheet could solve the problem. Problems should then be discussed with the entire class, and suggestions from students shared and considered. Ability to draw is not important; the students can describe their drawings or give a verbal answer.

To the student: You are going to see pictures of children in a class who are having some sort of problem. I want you to think about how each child could solve the problem and draw a picture of what he or she might do. Don't worry if you can't draw very well, because we will be sharing our pictures and our ideas, and you can tell us about your picture. There might be lots of ways each child could get out of the problem, so think about different things that child could do.

Answers

Answers will vary, although some common solutions may include:
- asking the teacher for help
- asking a friend for help
- replacing a missing object by buying or borrowing another one
- making a phone call to mom or dad
- finding sommething else to do until the problem situation changes

PROVIDING SOLUTIONS (4)

Problem	A solution
Someone is sitting in Karen's seat.  	
Allison broke her toy doll. 	
Steven needs to staple his papers, but there are no staples. 	
The gerbil got out of its cage. 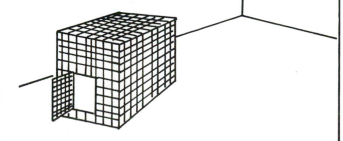	

II-23 PROVIDING SOLUTIONS (5)

Objective: The student will identify and explain the problem and provide an appropriate solution when presented with a problem situation.

Directions

To the teacher: The student will be presented with a problem. He or she will first identify the problem (written on the picture), and draw a picture that shows how the child on the worksheet could solve the problem. Problems should then be discussed with the entire class, and suggestions from students shared and considered. Ability to draw is not important; the students can describe their drawings or give a verbal answer.

To the student: You are going to see pictures of children in a class who are having some sort of problem. I want you to think about how each child could solve the problem and draw a picture of what he or she might do. Don't worry if you can't draw very well, because we will be sharing our pictures and our ideas, and you can tell us about your picture. There might be lots of ways each child could get out of the problem, so think about different things that child could do.

Answers

Answers will vary, although some common solutions may include:
- asking the teacher for help
- asking a friend for help
- replacing a missing object by buying or borrowing another one
- making a phone call to mom or dad
- finding something else to do until the problem situation changes

NAME _____   DATE _____

PROVIDING SOLUTIONS (5)

Problem	A solution
Sally is missing her sweater.	
Randy forgot to get a napkin at lunch.	
Rick wants to use the computer, but someone else is using it.	
Barbara hurt her leg outside on the playground.	

II-24 SOMETHING GOOD, SOMETHING BAD

Objective: The student will provide one or more positive and negative aspects of a given situation.

Directions

To the teacher: The student will be presented with situations that could be either good or bad. He or she is going to draw a picture of how that situation could be good (or fun) *and* how that same situation may not be good. After students have completed the activity, ideas should be shared. Each student should be able to state at least one positive and one negative aspect of the situation.

To the student: On this worksheet, you are going to think about something good that could happen or something fun you might do if it happened to you. Then, I want you to draw a picture that shows how that is a good thing. After that, I want you to think about how the same sitaution may not be good, or something that might not be fun about it, and draw a picture of that. We will talk about our pictures after everyone has finished. See how many ideas we can come up with.

Situations and Suggested Answers

	(good)	(bad)
A Rainy Day	fun to get wet	might ruin a baseball game
Being a New Student	fun to get to know new people	scary not knowing where things are
Being First in Line	you don't have to wait for slow people in front of you	you do have to wait for everyone else to get in line behind you

NAME _____   DATE _____

SOMETHING GOOD, SOMETHING BAD

	Something good	Something bad
A rainy day.		
Being a new student.		
Being first in line.		

II-25 POSITIVE AND NEGATIVE

Objective: The student will provide one or more positive and negative aspects of a given situation.

Directions

To the teacher: The student will be presented with several situations that have positive and negative aspects. He or she is to draw a picture showing how that situation could be good and how the same situation could be bad. After students have completed this activity, ideas should be shared. Each student should be able to state at least one positive and one negative aspect of the situation.

To the student: On this sheet, you are going to think about the situation shown, and try to think of something good about it and something bad about it. Then I want you to draw a picture showing your ideas. We will talk about our pictures and ideas after everyone has finished.

Situations and Suggested Answers

	(good)	*(bad)*
Learning a New Game in P.E.	might be a lot more fun than some old games	have to listen to rules about how to play before you can play
Wearing Glasses	you can see!	you have to be careful not to break or lose them
Listening to the Teacher Read Someone Else's Story Instead of Yours	it might be a really good story	you have to wait for the teacher to read yours at a different time

POSITIVE AND NEGATIVE

	Something good	Something bad
Learning a new game in P.E.		
Wearing glasses.		
Listening to the teacher read someone else's story instead of yours.		

II-26 PRETEND YOU ARE...AN ANIMAL

Objective: The student will answer the questions posed when presented with the task of imagining himself or herself to be something or someone else.

Directions

To the teacher: The student will select one animal on the worksheet that he or she would like to pretend to be. It may be helpful for your student to put a circle around that animal on the worksheet, to remember his or her choice. The student will then orally, or in writing if desired, respond to the questions that refer to qualities about animals as if he or she were that animal. This activity may be varied by having the student keep the choice a secret until the questions have been posed and other students have had a chance to guess which animal was selected.

To the student: We are going to pretend that you have changed yourself into one of the animals you see on this page. Put a circle around the animal you would like to pretend to be. Now I want you to answer the questions at the bottom of the page as if you were the animal you chose. When everyone is through, we will take turns answering the questions, and compare our answers.

Answers

Answers will vary. Encourage creativity within the bounds of the animal's usual limitations; for example, a fish would probably not sleep in a bed, but its favorite game might be playing school. A bat might not eat cereal for breakfast, but its response to a hungry lion might be: "I'm not going to hang around here anymore. Good bye!"

PRETEND YOU ARE...AN ANIMAL

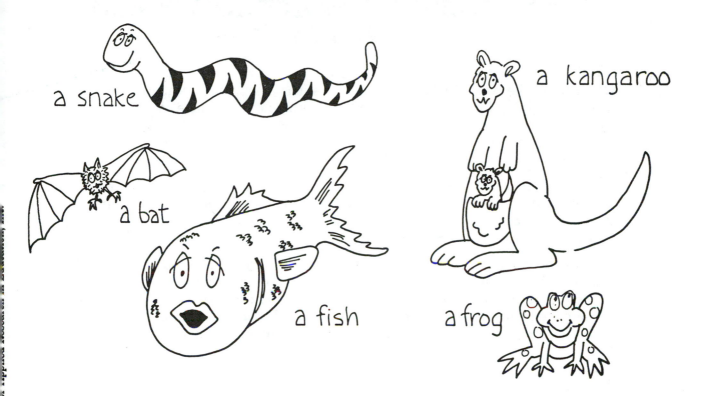

a snake

a kangaroo

a bat

a fish

a frog

1. Where do you sleep?

2. What do you eat for breakfast?

3. How do you move around?

4. What would you do if a lion came up to you and said, "I'm hungry."?

5. What's your favorite game?

6. What would make you happy?

7. What would make you sad?

II-27 PRETEND YOU ARE...ANOTHER PERSON

Objective: The student will answer the questions posed when presented with the task of imagining himself or herself to be something or someone else.

Directions

To the teacher: The student will select one person he or she would like to pretend to be, and circle it on the worksheet—then orally, or in writing, answer the questions as if he or she were that person. Students in the class can take turns listening to each other's responses.

To the student: Today you are going to pretend you have changed yourself into one of the people you see on this page. Put a circle around the person you would like to pretend to be. Now I want you to answer the questions at the bottom of the page as if you were the person you circled. When everyone is finished, we will take turns answering the questions, and compare our answers.

Answers

Answers will vary. Encourage creativity.

PRETEND YOU ARE...ANOTHER PERSON

a baby

a clown

a zookeeper

an astronaut

Santa Claus

1. What clothes do you wear to work or during the day?

2. How do you get to work?

3. What kind of pet do you like?

4. What would you say if a shoe salesperson asked what kind of shoes you want?

5. What would you like to eat for a snack?

6. What would be a good Christmas present for you?

II-28 PRETEND YOU ARE...AN OBJECT

Objective: The student will answer the questions posed when presented with the task of imagining himself or herself to be something or someone else.

Directions

To the teacher: The student will select one object pictured on the worksheet that he or she would like to pretend to be and answer the questions at the bottom of the page as if he or she were that object. Discuss the questions orally when everyone has finished.

To the student: Now I want you to pretend to be one of the objects you see on this page. Put a circle around the object you'd like to be. Now I want you to think about how you would answer the questions at the bottom of the page if you were that object. When everyone is through, we will take turns answering the questions and compare our answers.

Answers

Answers will vary.

PRETEND YOU ARE...AN OBJECT

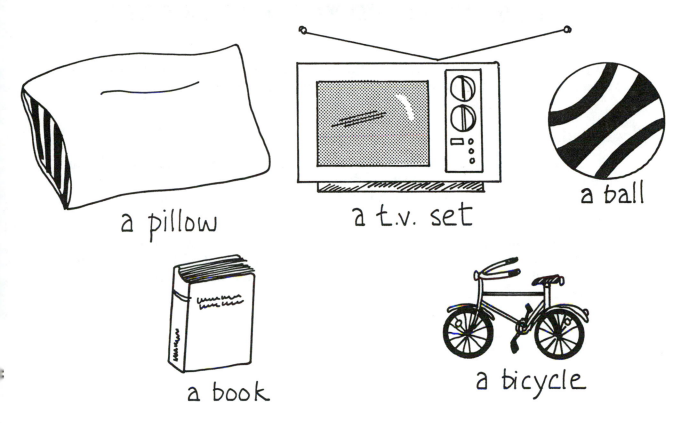

a pillow

a t.v. set

a ball

a book

a bicycle

1. Where should someone go to get you?

2. How much would you cost?

3. If you were broken, where would you go to be fixed?

4. Who would like to have you for a birthday present?

5. If you were left out in the rain, what would happen to you?

II-29   PRETEND YOU ARE...FOOD

Objective: The student will answer the questions posed when presented with the task of imagining himself or herself to be something or someone else.

Directions

To the teacher: The student will select one food item he or she would like to pretend to be and circle it. Each student will then answer the questions at the bottom of the page as if he or she were that food item. Discuss the questions orally when everyone has finished.

To the student: I want you to pretend to be one of the food items you see pictured on this sheet. Put a circle around it. Now I want you to answer the questions at the bottom as if you were that thing. When we're all finished, we'll compare our answers.

Answers

Answers will vary.

PRETEND YOU ARE...FOOD

a pizza

popcorn

candy

an ice cream cone

lemonade

peas

1. Where do you stay most of the time?

2. How does it feel when someone is eating you?

3. What is done to you to get you ready to be eaten?

4. What are you made of or where do you come from?

5. Where would someone find you in a store?

6. If you could talk, what would you say to someone who was going to eat you?

ENRICHMENT ACTIVITIES

"WHY" QUESTION activities (II-1 through II-3) can be extended by having students bring in pictures from magazines or newspapers that have interesting events depicted. The pictures can be displayed, the question "WHY?" can serve as the caption, and students can take turns either writing or verbally telling what they think might have caused the event to happen.

Another WHY activity is simply continuing to pose the question "Why?" after the student has made a comment, and seeing how far you can go before the student has run out of answers. For example, the student may come in and say, "I had an awful bus ride." You could counter with, "Why?" He may say, "I had to sit next to Billy." You: "Why?" Student: "Because he always sits near me." You: "Why?" Student: "Because he likes me!" You: "Why?" Student: "Because I'm so charming." You: "Why?" Student: "Because my parents brought me up right," etc., etc. This can be fun as the student tries to think of responses to keep the questions coming.

THE NEXT EVENT (II-7 through II-8) and *SEQUENCING activities (II-9 through II-11)* can be extended by making puzzles involving at least three events or parts. For example, the student may draw three pictures of getting ready to go out for recess, playing at recess, and coming in from recess. The pictures can then be cut apart, shuffled, and traded with other students to see if other people can sequence the event correctly.

MISSING INFORMATION (II-12 through II-13) can be emphasized in the classroom by giving obviously incomplete directions to students so that they have to ask for more information. Examples may include: "Everyone, get out your book." (which book?) "Take out your scissors and cut." (Cut what?) "Turn in your books to the right page." (Which page would that be?)

MAKING INFERENCES (II-14 through II-16) can be extended by using pictures from magazines or newspapers (or even drawings, if they are clear enough) that depict an event. The pictures can be cut in half (for example, *the man walking* on one side, *the bus that he is walking to* on the other side). Display only one side of the picture, and have students attempt to figure out what might be on the other side. Then show students the completed picture. Save these pictures for...

MULTIPLE CAUSES (II-17 through II-18) —display only one side of the picture while having students list several possible causes or "things that could be on the other side of the picture." In the above example, students may guess that the man is walking to a house, to meet another person, walking to get into a taxi, and so forth. Likewise, displaying only the bus may elicit responses such as a man walking to the bus, a woman walking to the bus, another car coming toward the bus, and so forth.

PROVIDING SOLUTIONS (II-19 through II-23) can be carried out all day through the classroom activities. When a trivial problem arises, you may wish to announce it to the class (as long as it does not embarrass any students) and open the floor for problem-solving solutions. For example, "Johnny can't find his reading book. Quick—tell me four things he could do!" The teacher may wish to keep a list on the chalkboard or other prominent place of problems that have arisen on any particular day. Then, at the end of the day or whatever time is suitable, the class can review the problems that came up and suggest solutions for them.

SOMETHING GOOD, SOMETHING BAD (II-24 through II-25) can be a fun, but mind-boggling experience when you try to think of good things about things that are normally thought of as negative, and vice versa. You might have the students list five bad things about homework (that's easy!), five good things about chocolate, five bad things about little brothers. THEN, have students try to turn them into the opposite characteristics: five good things about homework, five bad things about chocolate, and five good things about little brothers. The students will probably conclude that very few things (if anything) are 100 percent good or bad, and that most events or items have elements of both.

PRETEND YOU ARE...(II-26 through II-29) can easily be extended by having students come up with their own ideas of what they would like to pretend to be—in any category. After mentioning why they have chosen that particular thing, they may wish to answer questions (posed by the class) as if they were that thing they had chosen. This could also be played as sort of a "What's My Line?" game, with students not revealing their identity except through their responses to the questions.

section III

ACTIVITIES TO HELP STUDENTS IMPROVE THEIR CONVERSATIONAL SKILLS

Pets

A SURPRISE !!!!

115

THE GOAL OF SECTION III IS

- To improve overall communication by demonstrating appropriate conversational skills at appropriate times.

This section provides over 27 activities that will help students learn about and practice conversational skills. These skills include: appropriately gaining the attention of others; taking turns in a conversation; starting, continuing, and terminating a conversation; and staying on the topic.

While these skills can be practiced and studied, a better test of the student's knowledge and ability in this area is his or her use of the skills in spontaneous talking and everyday conversations with others. Role playing is suggested as a teaching technique on many of the activities because it simulates the situations the students will encounter; however, you are encouraged to allow time in class for opportunity to practice these skills spontaneously.

Re: Improving conversational skills

Dear Parents,

The next area of language we will be practicing in the classroom is that of carrying on a conversation. Your child will be learning and practicing ways to talk and listen to others by gaining attention properly; taking turns in a conversation; starting, continuing, changing, and ending conversations; and staying on the topic through a conversation. Look for papers from school with specific hints and techniques that we will be using at school to practice these skills.

At school, we will be role-playing (acting out) conversations and taking advantage of daily situations to use these conversational skills. At home, you will have different opportunities for your child to talk to others. For example, grandma coming for a visit, the next-door neighbor returning a cup of sugar, the mail carrier dropping off letters, seeing an acquaintance in the supermarket, occasional visits from relatives, and just sitting around the dinner table with the family.

You can help your child become a better conversationalist by taking note of the areas in which he or she has difficulty, and looking for opportunities to practice, practice, practice!

Sincerely,

_____

Teacher

III-1   GAINING ATTENTION

Objective: The student will gain the attention of others in a manner appropriate to each situation in which it is assessed.

Directions

To the teacher: The student will look at three situations in which children want to gain the attention of other children. One child is gaining attention in an appropriate manner; another child is not. The student is to put a circle around the child who is getting attention in an appropriate manner for the situation, and an X on the child in the picture who is not. Discuss why the manner of attention-getting is appropriate or inappropriate for that situation.

To the student: You are going to look at three situations. In each situation, there is one child who is getting attention from others in an appropriate manner. That means, what he or she is doing to get others to notice him or her is OK. There is one child in each situation who is not getting attention the right way. I want you to put a circle around the child who is getting attention the right way, and put an X on the child who is not. Then we'll talk about your answers.

Situations and Answers

1. Walking into a classroom
   appropriate—child saying "Good morning"
   inappropriate—child yelling "I'm here"
2. Talking in front of a group
   appropriate—child asking interesting question
   inappropriate—child hitting another on the head, saying "Stop talking"
3. Passing a friend in the hall
   appropriate—smiling to acknowledge friend
   inappropriate—extending hand to be slapped and yelling

GAINING ATTENTION

1.

III-2   NOTICE ME!

Objective: The student will gain the attention of others in a manner appropriate to each situation in which it is assessed.

Directions

To the teacher: The student will examine three situations in which two children want to gain the attention of their teacher. One child is gaining attention appropriately; the other is not. Students are to put a circle around the appropriately behaving child and put an X on the one who is not. Discuss why the manner of attention-getting is appropriate or inappropriate in these settings.

To the student: You are going to look at three situation. Two children are trying to get the attention of their teacher, Mrs. Jones. One child is getting attention in an appropriate way, and I want you to put a circle around that child. The other is getting attention in an inappropriate way, so I want you to put an X on that child. Then we'll talk about our reasons for these answers.

Situations and Answers

1. Teacher giving a lesson
   appropriate—child raising hand
   inappropriate—child yelling for teacher
2. Teacher walking around the room and helping children
   appropriate—child raising hand
   inappropriate—child sitting at desk and waiting to be noticed
3. Teacher working at desk
   appropriate—child tapping teacher on shoulder
   inappropriate—child throwing wad of paper at teacher

NOTICE ME!

1.

2.

3.

III-3   WHICH IS APPROPRIATE?

Objective: The student will gain the attention of others in a manner appropriate to each situation in which it is assessed.

Directions

To the teacher: The student will look at three situations in which children are attempting to gain the attention of a peer, a teacher in the classroom, and a teacher on the playground. The student is to circle the child who is gaining attention appropriately, and to put an X on the child who is not. Discuss why the manner of attention-getting is appropriate or inappropriate for that situation.

To the student: You are going to look at three situations in which children are trying to get the attention of someone. I want you to circle the one child in each situation who is getting attention in the most appropriate way, and to put an X on the one child in each situation who is not getting attention in the most appropriate way. Then we'll talk about your answers.

Situations and Answers

1. Children getting attention of another child
   appropriate—asking a question and looking at the other person
   inappropriate—talking while not looking at the other person
2. Teacher walking around room asking who has finished the reading assignment
   appropriate—raising hand
   inappropriate—slamming book
3. Children getting attention of teacher on the playground
   appropriate—child running up to teacher
   inappropriate—child yelling across playground

WHICH IS APPROPRIATE?

1.

2.

3.

III-4   LET OTHERS TALK, TOO

Objective: The students will take turns in conversations appropriately.

Directions

To the teacher: The students will read or listen to a conversation between Tom and Beth. You may want to have the students preview this activity sheet and take turns reading the parts of Tom and Beth and eventually role play this situation. Explain to the students that they are going to try to figure out if this is a conversation in which the people took turns talking. Tell the students you will also be asking them questions. (Students may circle their responses or respond orally.)

To the student: Today we are going to listen in on a conversation between two children, Tom and Beth. After hearing the conversation, I want you to tell me if the children were taking turns or not. There will then be five questions I will ask you to help us figure out if taking turns is important.

1. Did Tom and Beth take turns talking? (**Answer:** no)
2. Who did all of the talking? (**Answer:** Tom)
3. What did Beth do? (**Answer:** leave)
4. Why? (Answers may vary, but may include Beth's being bored or being tired of waiting for Tom to give her a chance to talk)
5. Why is it important to take turns when talking to someone else? (**Answer:** so the other person will stay interested in what you say)

NAME _____

DATE _____

LET OTHERS TALK, TOO

TOM

BETH

Hi Beth, would you like to see my new car?

My dad and I got it at the drug store.

We saw red ones and black ones, but I wanted to get the green one.

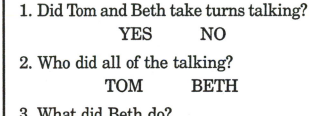

I'm going to play outside with this car at recess. Where are you going Beth?

1. Did Tom and Beth take turns talking?
   YES   NO

2. Who did all of the talking?
   TOM   BETH

3. What did Beth do? _____

4. Why? _____

5. Why is it important to take turns when talking to someone else? _____

_____

III-5   DON'T LEAVE SOMEONE OUT

Objective: The students will take turns in conversation appropriately.

Directions

To the teacher: The students will read or listen to a conversation among three people—Charles, Kay, and Michael. You may want to have the students preview this activity sheet and take turns reading and/or role playing the parts. Explain to the students that they are going to try to figure out if this is a conversation in which everyone is taking turns. They will then have questions to answer.

To the student: This time, we are going to listen in on a conversation among three children—Charles, Kay, and Michael. After hearing the conversation, I want you to tell me whether the children were taking turns. I will ask four questions to help us figure out if taking turns is important in this situation.

1. Did Charles, Kay, and Michael take turns talking? (**Answer:** no)
2. Circle the names of the two children who were doing all of the talking. (**Answer:** Charles and Kay)
3. How do you think Michael felt? (**Answer:** sad, left out, ignored, unimportant)
4. What is important to learn about taking turns when there are three people in a conversation? (**Answer:** give everyone a chance to talk, include everybody)

DON'T LEAVE SOMEONE OUT

CHARLES   **KAY**   **MICHAEL**

Hi, you guys. Did you watch that baseball game last night on t.v.?

Yes, I saw it! What a good game!

I didn't see the game. I got a new bike last night for my birthday!

I like baseball. I would like to go to a game sometime.

Me too. I like to play football too. Charles, do you?

I have a football at home.

Why don't you bring it to school tomorrow, Charles? We can play.

1. Did Charles, Kay, and Michael take turns talking?

         YES   NO

2. Circle the names of the two children who talked to each other:

   CHARLES   KAY   MICHAEL

3. How do you think the other child felt?

   _____

   _____

4. What is important to learn about taking turns when there are three people in a conversation? _____

   _____

III-6   PRACTICE TAKING TURNS

Objective: The students will take turns in conversations appropriately.

Directions

To the teacher: Students will pick (or be assigned) a partner with whom they will practice taking turns in a conversation. Topics to converse about are suggested on the worksheet: pets, books, favorite TV show, my sister, pizza, a surprise. After practicing, students will present their conversations in front of the class, being careful to take turns. Other students will decide whether the people were taking turns and discuss why or why not. Variations may include having groups of three children and having some groups specifically assigned to portray *not* taking turns. You may wish to tape record the conversations for analysis with the children.

To the student: Today I am going to have you work in small groups of two or three. You are going to practice taking turns in a conversation while the rest of us listen carefully to decide whether we think you are taking turns. On this page, you will see some ideas of things you could talk about with your partner. Put a circle around the topic you would like to talk about and I will assign you to your group.

NAME _____   DATE _____

III-6

PRACTICE TAKING TURNS

Pets

A Good Book

My Favorite T.V. Show

My Sister

PIZZA

A SURPRISE !!!!

III-7 HOW TO START A CONVERSATION

Objective: The student will demonstrate an understanding of how parts of a conversation are related through the use of conversation starters.

Directions

To the teacher: This is a discussion page in which the student is introduced to starting a conversation. The top part of the page lists suggestions for starting a conversation with someone you know. The bottom part of the page lists suggestions for starting a conversation with someone you may not know. Discuss these suggestions with students and have them give examples. You may wish to have students role-play these situations in front of the class.

To the student: Today we are going to start talking about the parts of a conversation. The first thing you need to know is how to start a conversation. This sheet gives some suggestions for starting a conversation with someone you know and someone you don't know. We're going to talk about these ideas, give examples, and practice some of them in front of the class.

HOW TO START A CONVERSATION

...with someone you know.

Talk about:

- things you both like to do

- what you did yesterday

- other people you both know

- what you are going to do

- something funny that happened

- a good book

- a good game

...with someone you don't know.

Find out:

- where he lives

- what he likes to do after school

- if he likes to draw

- if he has any pets

- his name

- if he has the same toys you have

III-8 WHERE DO I START?

Objective: The student will demonstrate an understanding of how parts of a conversation are related through the use of conversation starters.

Directions

To the teacher: On this sheet and the following two sheets (III-9 and III-10), the student is presented with a cartoon panel depicting a child who is starting a conversation. The student is given a suggestion for starting the conversation, and then is to write or copy the starting sentence or question in the balloon. You may wish to conduct this as a group activity and list the students' responses on the chalkboard so that they can copy their choice onto the paper. Another alternative is to have the students work in small groups and circulate among them, copying their choice on the paper. *Note:* You may wish to save these sheets for use with the next skill, *Continuing a Conversation,* in which the students will follow the starting sentence with a continuing sentence.

To the student: Today we are going to work on starting a conversation. In each of the four pictures, a child needs to think of a starting sentence to get the conversation going. I will tell you some clues as to what the child wants to talk about, and then I want you to give suggestions for what he or she could say. I will copy your suggestions on the board, and then I want you to pick one and write/copy/have it written on your paper.

Situations and Suggested Answers

1. Geoffrey wants to know how you are today. "How are you?" "How are you today?" "Do you feel good today?"
2. Sandy is interested in your dress. "Where did you get that dress?" "I like your dress." "Is that a new dress?"
3. Mike wants to know about your weekend. "What did you do this weekend?" "Did you go away this weekend?" "Tell me what you did this weekend."
4. Jenny wants to know what you're going to do tonight. "What are you doing tonight?" "Are you going anywhere tonight?"

132

NAME _____   *DATE* _____

WHERE DO I START?

1.

2.

3.

4.

III-9   WHICH WOULD YOU START WITH?

Objective: The student will demonstrate an understanding of how parts of a conversation are related through the use of conversation starters.

Directions

To the teacher: The student will supply a starting sentence for four contrived situations. Responses may be written or copied from the board onto the paper.

To the student: Today we are going to work some more on starting conversations. On this sheet, there are four situations in which children want to start a conversation with someone. I want you to think of some good starting sentences and then pick one you want to have on your paper.

Situations and Suggested Answers

1. Marcy, Jane, and Kathy see Ellen walking to school alone. "Would you like to walk with us?" "Are you going to school?" "Would you like to join us?" "May we walk with you?"
2. Dick is interested in what Janell is drawing on her paper. "May I see what you're drawing?" "Are you drawing a horse?" "What are you drawing?"
3. Lynn wants to know if the new boy in school has any brothers or sisters. "Do you have any brothers or sisters?" "Are you the only kid in your family?"
4. Fred wants David to know that his birthday is coming up soon. "It's my birthday tomorrow." "Guess what day tomorrow is for me?" "Tomorrow is my birthday."

WHICH WOULD YOU START WITH?

1.

2.

3.

4.

III-10 STARTING A CONVERSATION

Objective: The student will demonstrate an understanding of how parts of a conversation are related through the use of conversation starters.

Directions

To the teacher: The student will supply a starting sentence for four contrived situations. Responses may be written or copied from the board onto the paper.

To the student: Today, we are going to work some more on starting conversations. There are four situations on this sheet in which children want to start a conversation with someone. I want you to think of some good starting sentences and then pick one you want to have on your paper.

Situations and Suggested Answers

1. Andrew wants to let Nancy know he got a new puppy. "Guess what I got last night?" "I got a new pet last night." "Do you like puppies, Nancy?"

2. Christine wants to know if Jane would like to taste her ice cream. "Do you like ice cream?" "Would you like to try some of this?" "Would you like a taste of this?"

3. Arnold wants to know if Ben watched TV yesterday. "Did you watch TV last night?" "Did you watch anything on TV yesterday?" "Did you watch that cowboy movie yesterday on TV?"

4. Alice wants to know what Mindy is reading. "Is that a good book?" "What book is that?" "I'd like to see that book when you're finished." "Could I see that?" "What are you reading?"

STARTING A CONVERSATION

1.

2.

3.

4.

III-11 HOW TO CONTINUE A CONVERSATION

Objective: The student will demonstrate an understanding of how parts of a conversation are related by continuing a topic.

Directions

To the teacher: This is a discussion page for introducing the student to *continuing* a conversation or topic of discussion. Two children are depicted on the page with one starting the conversation, and then both children contributing to keeping the conversation going. This may be demonstrated by having students take turns reading the worksheet or by role playing.

To the student: Today we are going to learn about what you do after a conversation has been started: you *continue* it. That means you keep on talking about what you started talking about. This page gives you some ideas about how to continue a conversation.

HOW TO CONTINUE A CONVERSATION

CONTINUING

First, I'll say something to you.

Then I will answer you.

Then I will say something else to you.

And I'll say something back to you.

Maybe I will ask you a question.

I'll answer your question, then maybe I'll ask you a question.

And I'll answer! How long do we keep doing this?

As long as we want to!

III-12   KEEP SAYING MORE

Objective: The student will demonstrate an understanding of how parts of a conversation are related by continuing a topic.

Directions

To the teacher: The student will practice continuing a topic by listening to or reading the first two sentences of a conversation in which one person starts and the second person continues. The student will supply a sentence that continues the conversation for the first person. You may wish to write suggested sentences on the board and have students select one to copy on their paper.

To the student: Today we will work a little more on continuing a conversation. Remember that the first person starts a conversation by asking a question or saying something interesting. Then the second person continues the conversation by saying something about what the first person said. Then the first person has a turn to talk again. (Remember what we learned about taking turns?) I want you to read/listen to these two conversations and help the first person think of something to say that continues the conversation.

Answers

Answers will vary, but typical responses may include:

1. Well, it's really different.
   I think the colors are pretty.
   Yes, I like it a lot.
   I love it; do they have any more?
2. Yes, I've been to several zoos.
   Yes, but it's been awhile.
   I went with my Boy Scout troop last summer.
   No, but I'd like to go. Was it fun?

KEEP SAYING MORE

1.

2.

III-13 CONTINUING THE CONVERSATION

Objective: The student will demonstrate an understanding of how parts of a conversation are related by continuing a topic.

Directions

To the teacher: The student will supply a sentence that continues a conversational topic between two children. You may wish to write suggested sentences on the board and have students select one to copy on their paper.

To the student: On this sheet, I want you to read/listen to the conversation going on and come up with a sentence to help the first person continue the conversation. I will write your ideas on the board and you can select the one you like.

Answers

Answers will vary, but typical responses may include:

1. I feel fine, too
   I feel great; we're going to a football game tonight.
   I'm a little tired because my brother and I stayed up late to watch a monster movie.
2. No, but tell me about it.
   Yes, and I liked it a lot.
   No, last night I had to go to my uncle's house.
   Yes, but I missed the ending. What happened?

CONTINUING THE CONVERSATION

1.

2.

III-14   KEEP IT GOING!

Objective: The student will demonstrate an understanding of how parts of a conversation are related by continuing a topic.

Directions

To the teacher: On this activity, the student will practice continuing a conversation by role playing with a partner or partners. Each student will pick one of the five topics listed on the worksheet and briefly rehearse with his or her partner(s). The role plays can be presented in front of the class. At this point, clear endings to the conversations are not necessary. You may wish to tape record the role plays and have the students analyze their conversations.

To the student: Today, you are going to get in small groups and practice starting and continuing a conversation with your partner(s). While you are giving your role play in front of the class, the rest of us will be listening to your conversation for good continuing sentences.

KEEP IT GOING!

Get a partner. How long can you keep this conversation going?

1. "What are you reading?"

2. "Do you have a bike?"

3. "Would you like to come to my house after school?"

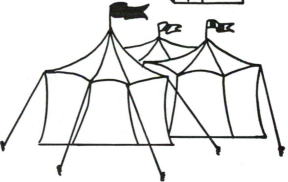

4. "Do you like to go to the circus?"

5. "Can you draw a sports car?"

III-15 HOW TO CHANGE THE TOPIC

Objective: The student will demonstrate an understanding of how parts of a conversation are related by changing a topic.

Directions

To the teacher: This is a discussion page to introduce the idea of changing a topic of conversation. This page suggests that a topic should be changed when (1) you've talked about one thing for a long time; (2) you are talking about something that makes someone feel bad; or (3) it is not the right time or place to talk about it. Have students discuss the examples presented on the page by asking them for reasons why the person listening may not be interested in what the first person is talking about. Ask students for more examples of topics that should be changed.

To the student: Now we are going to start talking about when you should change a topic of conversation. There are several reasons why it might be a good idea to stop talking about what you're talking about and switch to something else. What ideas do you get from looking at the person who's talking? What ideas do you get from the person who's listening?

Answers

1. The girl has been talking about dogs for a long time. The other girl is not interested in the conversation anymore.
2. The boy is talking about something bloody and scary. The other boy doesn't like hearing about bloody things.
3. The boy is talking about how they did on a test. The girl did not do very well on the test, feels bad about it, and does not want to talk about it right now.

HOW TO CHANGE THE TOPIC

Talk about something else when:

1. You've talked about one thing for a long time and the other person has nothing to say about it.

2. You are talking about something that makes someone else feel bad.

3. It is not the right time or place to talk about it.

III-16   SHOULD I CHANGE THE TOPIC?

Objective: The student will demonstrate an understanding of how parts of a conversation are related by changing a topic.

Directions

To the teacher: On this page, the student will read or listen to a situation in which someone is talking about a topic that may or may not be exhausted, offensive, or inappropriate at that time. The student is to think about the situation and decide whether he or she would change the topic to something else and what reasons exist for changing the topic. In some cases, it is truly a matter of student discretion whether to change the topic or not. Be sure to allow time for discussion of responses, since there will be variance of opinion; however, it is of greater importance that the student be able to express an opinion than to simply guess yes or no on a topic. Students can circle their responses for each item.

To the student: We have been talking about when you should change a topic to something else. Do you remember some of the reasons we talked about for changing a topic to something else? (Review *How to Change the Topic*, Activity III-15). Now I want you to think about some topics that are on your paper and decide whether you would change the topic to something else and *why* or perhaps decide *when* you would change the topic. There really are no right or wrong answers, but I want you to think about the situations and tell the rest of us what you think about it. You can indicate whether you would change the topic by circling YES or NO or MAYBE on your paper.

Answers

These are suggested responses; however, individual answers may vary according to situations (which should be explained by the students to justify their answers).

1. No (unless the other person is bored)
2. Yes (embarrassing topic for Mary)
3. Yes (makes someone feel bad)
4. No
5. Yes (makes someone feel bad)
6. Yes (not the right time)
7. No
8. Yes (not the right time)
9. Yes (not the right time)
10. No (personal opinion)

SHOULD I CHANGE THE TOPIC?

1. You are talking about your birthday party. Everyone in the class is invited to come.

   YES   NO   MAYBE

2. You are talking about Mary's dirty dress. She fell down on the playground in the mud and can't go home to change clothes.

   YES   NO   MAYBE

3. You are talking about how big Johnny's ears are.

   YES   NO   MAYBE

4. You and a friend are talking about a movie you both went to see.

   YES   NO   MAYBE

5. You are telling a friend about a bloody accident you saw on TV, but your friend doesn't like bloody things.

   YES   NO   MAYBE

6. You are asking a friend to go to the circus with you, but he doesn't have any money because his family is very poor.

   YES   NO   MAYBE

7. You are talking with a friend about how you feel about taking a math test.

   YES   NO   MAYBE

8. You are talking about your new kitten to a friend whose cat just got hit by a car.

   YES   NO   MAYBE

9. You are talking about how the ketchup on your hot dog looks like blood.

   YES   NO   MAYBE

10. You are talking about how you can't stand to eat green beans.

    YES   NO   MAYBE

III-17   SOME TOPIC CHANGERS

Objective: The student will demonstrate an understanding of how parts of a conversation are related by changing a topic.

Directions

To the teacher: This is a discussion page in which students are introduced to ways to change a topic that may be worn out or inappropriate. Have students look at the pictures and try to figure out why the topic should be changed, what the listener changed the topic to, and how the listener might have effected this change.

To the student: Sometimes when you are having a conversation with someone, you may want to change the topic to something else. Why might you want to do that? (Review III-15 and III-16). This page shows three ways that you could change a topic. Let's look at them and see if you can figure out *why* the listener wanted to change the topic, *what* the listener changed the topic to, and *how* the listener said or did something to let the first person know that he or she wanted to talk about something else.

Answers

Answers may vary, but suggested responses include:

1. Why: speaker was dominating conversation with bikes.
   What: listener changed to talking about one of her interests, tennis.
   How: listener might have said something like: "You really know a lot about bicycles. Do you know anything about tennis?"
2. Why: listener perhaps not interested in hearing about an accident.
   What: listener did not really change topic, but gave no reason to continue.
   How: the listener was silent.
3. Why: listener did not want to talk about Johnny's big ears.
   What: listener changed topic to earrings.
   How: listener asked a question *somewhat* related.

SOME TOPIC CHANGERS

Show you want to change the topic by:

1. Talking about something else.

2. Not saying anything.

3. Asking a question about something else.

III-18   IS THIS A GOOD CONVERSATION?

Objective: The student will demonstrate an understanding of how parts of a conversation are related by a topic.

Directions

To the teacher: The students will read or listen to a conversation between two children, Bob and Debby. After they have heard the conversation, you will ask them questions about starting, continuing, and changing the conversation. Make sure the students understand what you mean when you refer to "Box 1," and so on, which refers to the number of the cartoon panel.

To the student: We are going to listen in on a conversation between two children, Bob and Debby. After you listen to this conversation, I am going to ask you some questions about how you think it went. Keep in mind some of the things we've been learning about starting, continuing, and changing a conversation.

1. Look at Box 1. Who started the conversation: (**Answer:** Bob)
2. What topic is he talking about? (**Answer:** bicycles)
3. In Box 2, how did Debby continue the conversation? (**Answer:** she asked a question)
4. In Box 3, how did Bob show he was listening to Debby? (**Answer:** he answered her question)
5. How did Debby change the conversation? (**Answer:** she talked about something else)
6. What did she change the topic to? (**Answer:** her pony)
7. In Box 4, did Bob seem to be interested in the new topic? (**Answer:** yes)
8. How did he show that? (**Answer:** he continued talking about the pony)
9. Was this a good conversation? (**Answer:** yes)

IS THIS A GOOD CONVERSATION?

III-19   WHAT WAS SAID?

Objective: The student will demonstrate an understanding of how parts of a conversation are related by changing a topic.

Directions

To the teacher: The students will read or listen to a conversation between two children, Mark and Kevin. After they have heard the conversation, you will ask them questions about starting, continuing, and changing the conversation. Students will need to know what "Box 1," "Box 2," and so on, refer to.

To the student: We are going to listen in on a conversation between two children, Mark and Kevin. After you listen to this conversation, I am going to ask you some questions about how you think it went. Remember things about starting, continuing, a changing a conversation. Let's see if this was a good conversation.

1. In Box 1, who started the conversation: (**Answer:** Mark)
2. How did he start it? (**Answer:** with a greeting and asking a question)
3. What was the topic? (**Answer:** softball)
4. In Box 2, did Kevin change or continue the topic? (**Answer:** continue)
5. What did Mark talk about in Boxes 3 and 4? (**Answer:** how badly Kevin played)
6. How did Kevin feel? (**Answer:** probably unhappy)
7. Should Mark or Kevin have changed the topic? (**Answer:** yes)
8. Why? (**Answer:** because the other person was made to feel unhappy)
9. What could Mark have said to change the topic? (**Answer:** talked about a different sport or talked about something Kevin does well)
10. What could Kevin have said or done to change the topic? (**Answer:** talked about something he does well or asked Mark a question about something else or walked away)
11. Was this a good conversation? (**Answer:** no)

WHAT WAS SAID?

III-20 MORE PRACTICE IN CHANGING THE TOPIC

Objective: The student will demonstrate an understanding of how parts of a conversation are related by changing a topic.

Directions

To the teacher: The students will practice role-playing, changing a topic in front of the class with a partner. They will select one of six topics listed on the page, and briefly rehearse with their partners before presenting their play in front of the class. The rest of the class should listen to the role play and give suggestions for ways to change the topic. You may wish to tape record the role plays for group or individual analysis.

To the student: Today you are going to have a partner and practice changing the topic with him. After you practice for awhile by yourselves, you will perform your role play in front of the class while we listen for good conversations. (Remember starting, continuing, and changing techniques?) Pick a topic on the page that you would like to talk about, and I will get you into a small group.

Suggested Topic Changers

1. I like dogs, too. Do you like cats?
2. Reading is fun. Have you read any books at the library?
3. I was really scared when I heard that noise. Then it turned out to be just a little bird. Were you ever scared for a silly reason?
4. Eating chocolate is my favorite thing to do. On my birthday, we had chocolate ice cream. Do you like birthdays?
5. I like rainy days because mom lets us make a tent in the living room with blankets. Do you play indoor games when it rains?
6. On Sunday, we'll go out to eat. What will you do on Monday?

MORE PRACTICE IN CHANGING THE TOPIC

1. Pick a partner.
2. Pick one of the topics below.
3. Practice changing the topic with your partner.
4. Then do your conversation in front of the class.
5. How did you do?

Start talking about: **Change the topic to:**

dogs    →   cats

what you like to read    →   going to the library

 something scary   →   something funny

 eating chocolate   →   a birthday party

a rainy day    →   indoor games

what you will do on Sunday   →   what you will do on Monday

III-21 HOW TO END A CONVERSATION

Objective: The student will demonstrate an understanding of how parts of a conversation are related by terminating a conversation.

Directions

To the teacher: This discussion page introduces ways to end a conversation. The page teaches that, in general, you should say something nice before leaving. Several examples are given with the suggestion to smile at the end. Discuss with students reasons why you should end a conversation nicely. You may wish to have students practice these sentences with each other in front of the class.

To the student: We are going to learn about ways to end a conversation. After you have been talking for awhile, you might want to stop talking. This page lists some ways you could end your conversation. Maybe you can think of some other ways, too. Why do you think it's important to end a conversation nicely and with a smile? (leaves a good impression, lets everyone know when the conversation is over).

HOW TO END A CONVERSATION

End a conversation by

SAYING SOMETHING  NICE

See you later!

It was nice talking to you!

Good-bye for now!

Bye Jimmy!

 Let's talk again soon.

Let's play again later!

 I'll look for you on the bus!

 See you tomorrow!

AND

SMILING!

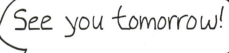

III-22 REASONS FOR ENDING A CONVERSATION

Objective: The student will demonstrate an understanding of how parts of a conversation are related by terminating a conversation.

Directions

To the teacher: This discussion page introduces appropriate times or situations for ending a conversation with someone. Not only does a person need to know *how* to end a conversation, he also needs to know under what conditions or situations the conversation should stop. Discuss with your students the four examples on the page (you have to go, your listener has to go, you've run out of things to say, you don't want to talk anymore) and why that would indicate it's time to end the conversation.

To the student: This page explains some situations when it's best to end a conversation. We're going to look at the situations, think about *why* that would be a good time to end the conversation, and think back to *ways* to end a conversation to come up with a good way to end each conversation.

Answers

Suggested responses include:

1. Why end conversation: you need to leave (mother calling you). Ways to end: "Sorry—I have to go now. See you later."
2. Why end conversation: the listener needs to leave (mother calling her). Ways to end: "Looks like I need to go, too. It was fun talking to you."
3. Why end conversation: have exhausted the topic, one or both people tired of talking, do not wish to change or continue topic. Ways to end: "See you later," "Goodbye," "We'll talk again later."
4. Why end conversation: it's not a good time to continue conversation. Ways to end: "I don't feel like talking right now," "I think I need to do something else, so I'll see you later."

REASONS FOR ENDING A CONVERSATION

1. You have to leave.

2. The other person has to leave.

3. You can't think of anything else to say.

4. You don't want to talk any more.

III-23 HOW WOULD YOU END THESE CONVERSATIONS?

Objective: The student will demonstrate an understanding of how parts of a conversation are related by terminating a conversation.

Directions

To the teacher: The student will be presented with four situations in which the child is ending a conversation. The student will think of a good way to end the conversation and write/copy his response in the balloon.

To the student: On this sheet, you will see four stories which show children who are ready to end a conversation. I will tell you about the situation, and I want you to think of how that child might say something nice to show the other person that the conversation is over. You can write your answer in the balloon to show what the child is saying or, after we have listed several ideas on the board, copy the answer that you want him or her to have.

Situations and Suggested Answers

1. Alex was talking to another boy about reading sports stories when he looked up and saw his father coming into the room. Alex wanted to end the conversation so he could leave with his dad. What could Alex say?

   Answers: There's my dad, I'll talk to you about that book later, OK?
   Thanks for telling me about that book. I'll tell my dad about it, because here he is!

2. Barbara and Cynthia were talking about their new necklaces while they were eating lunch. Then Cynthia decided she'd like to end the conversation so she could go back to class. What could Cynthia say?

   Answer: I do like your necklace! I'll have to see it later 'cause I'm in a hurry to go back to class now.

3. Ricky just came back from the dentist where he had two teeth pulled. His jaw hurts a lot and he doesn't feel like talking to Billy about playing baseball after school. What could he say to let Billy know why he wants to end the conversation?

   Answer: I'd really like to talk to you about baseball, but my mouth hurts a lot and I don't think I'll be playing. See you later.

4. Steve and Randy were playing checkers until Randy's bus came and he had to get on it. What could Steve say to Randy to end their talk about the game?

   Answer: We'll play again tomorrow! 'Bye!

162

HOW WOULD YOU END THESE CONVERSATIONS?

1.

2.

3.

4.

III-24   HOW TO STAY ON THE TOPIC

Objective: The student will demonstrate coherence in a conversation by maintaining relevancy.

Directions

To the teacher: This is a discussion page to introduce relevancy (or "making sense") in a conversation. The comment at the top of the page tells the student: When you ask or tell something, it should *make sense*. The first example shows two children who are having separate conversations. The only thing in common is the word "red." The second child is acting as though she never heard a word of the first child's sentence. The second example shows two children carrying on a relevant conversation. Both children are talking about the same topic: kickball. When you discuss this page, make sure the students realize the difference between staying on the topic and changing the topic. Techniques for changing a topic (talking about something else, not saying anything, asking a question about something else) may sound similar to conducting a conversation without staying on the topic. However, the difference is that generally you should stay on the topic unless there is a *reason* to change (exhausting one topic, talking about something that makes someone feel unhappy, talking about something at an inappropriate time or place). The students are to assume that the activities for this section involve conversational topics that should *not* be changed.

To the student: Another important thing to remember about carrying on a conversation is to make sense. When someone says something to you, you should continue the conversation by saying something back that shows you were listening and interested. You can do this by making sense. We will look at two examples and see if the conversation makes sense or not.

HOW TO STAY ON THE TOPIC

When you ask or tell something, it should make sense.

This does not make sense...

This does...

III-25 WHICH MAKE SENSE?

Objective: The student will demonstrate coherence in a conversation by maintaining relevancy.

Directions

To the teacher: The student will read or listen to three situations in which one child is asking another a question or making a comment about something. The second child is to maintain relevancy by giving a response that stays on the topic. The student will have four answers to pick from, but only two of them maintain relevancy. The student is to put a check mark in front of the two answers with which the second child could respond to stay on the topic.

To the student: Who remembers what staying on the topic means? On this page, you are going to look at three situations in which a child is saying something to another child. The second child is going to say something back, but it has to make sense. There are four answers to pick from, but only two of them could make sense by staying on the topic. I want you to (read/listen to) the answers and put a check mark in the box in front of the two answers that would make sense in this conversation. When we're finished, we'll talk about why some of the answers stayed on the topic and others didn't.

Answers

1. a,b
2. b,c
3. a,d

NAME _____   DATE _____

III-25

WHICH MAKE SENSE?

1.

Did you get your homework done?

□ a. Yes, I got it done.

□ b. No, I didn't have time.

□ c. I don't feel good.

□ d. What time is it?

2.

We played baseball last night.

□ a. I have a football.

□ b. Who did you play with?

□ c. Did your team win?

□ d. Let's eat.

3.

I like to watch cartoons on TV.

□ a. Which cartoons do you watch?

□ b. My brother got new shoes.

□ c. My mom has a radio.

□ d. I saw some cartoons last night.

III-26   STAY ON THE TOPIC!

Objective: The student will demonstrate coherence in a conversation by maintaining relevancy.

Directions

To the teacher: The student will read or listen to three situations in which one child is asking another a question or making a comment about something. The second child is to maintain relevancy by giving a response that stays on the topic. The student will pick the two responses from the four given that are relevant or stay on the topic.

To the student: On this page, you are going to look at three situations again and help the second child stay on the topic. Two out of the four answers given could be right. The other two are different topics or don't make sense. I want you to read/listen to the answers and put a check mark in the box in front of the two answers that would make sense in this conversation. When we're through, we'll talk about why some of the answers made sense and the others weren't on the topic.

Answers

1. a, c
2. b, d
3. c, d (Make sure students understand that the underlined words indicate the title of a book.)

STAY ON THE TOPIC!

1.

What's your dog's name?

☐ a. Ginger.

☐ b. I have a cat, too.

☐ c. We haven't named her yet.

☐ d. Do you like dogs?

2.

We got a new car last night.

☐ a. We got a new refrigerator last night.

☐ b. What kind of car?

☐ c. My uncle went fishing with us.

☐ d. I'd like to see your car sometime.

3.

What library book are you reading?

☐ a. I'm getting my hair cut.

☐ b. We're going shopping after school.

☐ c. Tom Thumb.

☐ d. I'm reading a book about Indians.

III-27 THAT MAKES SENSE

Objective: The student will demonstrate coherence in a conversation by maintaining relevancy.

Directions

To the teacher: The student will read or listen to three situations in which one child is asking another a question or making a comment about something. The second child is to maintain relevancy by giving a response that stays on the topic. The student will pick the two responses from the four given that are relevant or stay on the topic.

To the student: You are going to look at three situations and help the second child stay on the topic started by the first. Two out of the four answers given could be right. The other two don't make sense or are a different topic. I want you to read/listen to the answers and put a check mark in the box in front of the two answers that would make sense in this conversation. When we're all finished, we'll talk about why some of the answers made sense and the others weren't staying on the topic.

Answers

1. b, c
2. a, b
3. b, c

THAT MAKES SENSE

1.

I like your shoes.

☐ a. I have a bandage on my toe.

☐ b. Thank you.

☐ c. I got them last week.

☐ d. May I use your pencil?

2.

Let's listen to some records.

☐ a. What records do you have?

☐ b. I like to listen to music.

☐ c. I want to go outside.

☐ d. Michael broke the puzzle.

3.

What did you do this weekend?
☐ a. I'm going to go outside now.

☐ b. I went fishing.

☐ c. I stayed home.

☐ d. Today is Monday.

ENRICHMENT ACTIVITIES

GAINING ATTENTION activities (III-1 through III-3) can be adapted for role-playing in the classrooms. Each situation could be portrayed twice, once demonstrating the appropriate way to gain attention in the situation and once demonstrating an inappropriate way.

TAKING TURNS (III-4 through III-6) can also be demonstrated by arranging the students in a circle and passing a small object, such as a beanbag, from student to student. The student currently in possession of the beanbag has the floor and it is his turn to talk until he tosses the beanbag to another student. You can vary the rules for tossing the beanbag; for example, after you've made one comment, after 15 seconds, and so forth.

STARTING A CONVERSATION (III-7 through III-10) can be extended by having children listen to other children in a relatively unstructured setting at school; for example, the lunchroom or the playground at recess. Assign them the task of listening to others starting conversations and remembering what their starting sentence was. The class can then compile a list of sentences, topics, or comments that typically are used in their school to start conversations. This can further be extended by devoting one classroom bulletin board to the "topic of the week." Huge lips on the bulletin board can be exclaiming, "HEY! LET'S TALK ABOUT...." with the topic of the week completing the sentence. For that week, students can concentrate on starting conversations with peers and friends from other classes. Any item of knowledge that a student wishes to share with the others about that topic can also be displayed on the bulletin board, giving the other students something else to talk about.

CONTINUING (III-11 through III-14) can be practiced as a circle game in which the conversation proceeds in one direction, with each child expected to continue talking about the topic given.

For further practice in continuing a topic, the worksheets from the previous skill, starting a conversation (III-8, III-9, and III-10), can be used. On these sheets, the student was requested to supply a starting sentence for a conversation. In the panel across from the starting sentence, the student can supply a continuing sentence for the second child in the picture. The same procedure—having students suggest several possible responses and selecting one—can be used. Sentences can be written on the board and copied by the students or teacher onto the students' papers. Following are suggested answers for this exercise.

Suggested Answers

III-8

1. How are you today?/I'm fine; how are you?
2. Where did you get that dress?/I got it at the dress shop. Do you like it?

172

3. What did you do this weekend?/I went camping. How about you?
4. What are you going to do tonight? I'm going to the park. What are you doing?

III-9

1. Would you like to walk with us?/Yes, do you live near here?
2. What are you drawing?/I'm drawing a dinosaur. Would you like to see it?
3. Do you have any brothers or sisters?/Yes, one sister. Do you?
4. It's my birthday tomorrow./Oh really? Are you doing anything special?

III-10

1. I got a new pet last night./What did you get?
2. Want some of my ice cream?/Sure, what flavor is it?
3. Did you watch TV last night?/Yes, what did you watch?
4. Is that a good book?/Yes, would you like to read it?

CHANGING THE TOPIC (III-15) through III-20) can be turned into a game activity by using a timer. Accept comments on a given topic until a timer set for small intervals of time goes off. Then the topic shifts to something else. Topics can be selected by polling students about their interests or picking general topics that your students have experience with.

ENDING A CONVERSATION (III-21 through III-23) can be extended as a class activity in which ending comments are written on brightly colored slips of construction paper and mounted around the room. Then, when students are consciously trying to end a conversation, they can scan the wall or room for a statement or comment that may be appropriate. Many endings to conversations are general enough that they would apply to a number of situations— "Nice talking to you," "See you later," "We can talk about this again later."

STAYING ON THE TOPIC (III-24 through III-27) can be practiced as a small group activity in which the teacher awards each student with a token or chip for making a comment that is relevant or on the topic given. This activity is most fun when performed quickly, such as in a two-minute drill. Topics may be written on paper, slipped into a bowl, and drawn out randomly. Whatever the topic is (making sure that all topics are such that the students have had experience with them), as long as the student makes a relevant comment, he or she will receive a chip. If a comment is not on the topic (at the teacher's discretion), the student will not receive a chip. Be sure to reinforce appropriate comments (quickly!) by praising the student. The two minutes will go fast, but the students will have to do some concentrating!

section IV

ACTIVITIES TO HELP STUDENTS WITH THEIR EVERYDAY COMMUNICATION SKILLS

THE GOAL OF SECTION IV IS

- To improve functional communication skills by
  appropriately obtaining and exchanging information with others.

This section provides activities designed to stimu-
late your students' awareness of and practice in using
everyday communication skills in order to obtain and
exchange information with others.

The first 12 activity pages involve naming, describing, and explaining activities. The next 7 activities deal
with describing past, present, and created events; and the
remaining 20 activity pages stress the appropriateness of
oral communication in a variety of situations.

A letter to parents is included at the beginning of
each main part, and enrichment activities are listed at
the end of the section.

The activities in Section IV are intended primarily
for oral expression, although having the students write
responses or draw pictures certainly can accompany and
enhance the oral lesson.

Re: Naming, describing, and explaining activities

Dear Parents,

    We will soon be starting another group of skills for language development in school. It's another area in which you can be a real help to your child at home: *everyday communication skills.*

    What are these skills? Simply learning how to *obtain* and *exchange information* with others. At school, the first group of skills we will be working on includes *labeling and describing objects, stating facts and opinions,* and *giving short explanations when answering questions.*

    At home, you can continue to emphasize these skills by asking your child to *name* and *describe* common household objects whenever possible (for example, spatula, ice-maker, quilt, bunkbed). Ask him or her to give an *opinion* about something (What do you think we should have for dinner? Do you think this soup is too hot?). Ask for·*facts* (What do you know about fire? Tell me about birds).

    Have your child answer your questions *completely.* If more information is needed (What are you doing? Playing.), prompt him or her by encouraging, "Tell me more. What are you playing?" Let your child know when you're satisfied: "Oh, now I understand! Thanks!"

    Communicating with others is one of the most important and efficient ways to obtain information. Lots of practice is going to help make it easier!

                      Sincerely,

                      _____

                      Teacher

IV-1 MY VACATION ON EARTH

Objective: The student will relate information meaningfully to others by labeling.

Directions

To the teacher: The student is to be introduced to Rizbo, a space creature (from the planet Uggot). This character will reappear in some future worksheets as a visitor who needs some clarification of English words and activities. On this activity, the student will read or listen to a story in which Rizbo describes his vacation on earth. Certain key words are omitted, but words describing the word appear and are underlined. The student is to try to think of the missing word and either volunteer to tell it orally or write it on the line next to the description.

To the student: You are going to read/hear a story about Rizbo, a creature from another planet named Uggot. As you will hear in the story, Rizbo has some trouble coming up with some words that we use everyday. When he gets to a word he can't remember, he describes it instead. I want you to try to think of the word he needs. Answers can be given orally or written on the lines.

Answers

1. lake, pond, ocean
2. shore
3. bicycle
4. road, street
5. ball
6. boy
7. bandage
8. house
9. kitchen
10. cookies
11. oven

MY VACATION ON EARTH

My name is Rizbo, and I am from the planet Uggot, which is a long, long way from your planet. One day I decided to take a short vacation to your planet. I had a good time, but I had some trouble remembering some of your words. Can you help me retell my story?

My spaceship landed in a large area of water (1)_____. I crawled out and swam to the side of this area of water (2)_____. Then I found a two-wheeled vehicle with handlebars and a seat (3)_____ and got on it. I pedaled down the place where cars travel (4)_____ and continued for quite a long way.

I was doing fine until I ran over a small, round object that is used to play games (5) _____ and fell off. A small male person (6)_____ came running up to me to ask if I was hurt. He said he would get me a tan, sticky covering to put over a sore spot (7) _____ if I wanted one. I didn't know what that was, so I said "Sure!"

I followed him to his small building with a mailbox in front (8)_____ where we went into the room with a refrigerator (9)_____. His mother came in and said, "Oh, you poor thing!" and gave me some sweet-tasting round things with chocolate chips in them (10)_____ right from the machine that cooks things (11)_____. I decided to spend the rest of my vacation right there!

IV-2 HOW MANY CAN YOU NAME?

Objective: The student will relate information meaningfully to others by **labeling**.

Directions

To the teacher: The students will generate oral or written lists of objects or other items that fit into the given category. You may want to have the students work in small groups on different categories, or, have the entire class try to generate lists together. An alternative idea is to have students who wish to, draw pictures of several of their ideas. You could list the items on the chalkboard or large paper, or do this as an oral, thinking activity.

To the student: In front of you is a list of 15 different categories, or groups of things. We are going to put our heads together and try to think of as many objects or items that fit into each group as we can.

Answers

Typical responses may include:

1. bike, motorcycle, tricycle
2. jacket, pencil, paper
3. sandwich, straw, napkin
4. nail polish, mittens, lotion
5. curly slide, swings, hopscotch lines
6. broom, extra paper, hangers
7. charcoal pencils, markers, paintbrush
8. gerbil cage, window, bookcase window
9. gerbil, hamster, guinea pig
10. radio, record player, piano
11. goldfish, paper towel, plants
12. TV set, computer, reading book pages
13. alphabet chart, a T-shirt, calendar
14. bike, pony, brother's back
15. gum, caramel, licorice

HOW MANY CAN YOU NAME?

1. Things that have wheels.

2. Things you need for school.

3. Things you would find in a lunchbox.

4. Things you put on your hands.

5. Things you would find on a playground.

6. Things you would find in a closet at school.

7. Things you can use to draw with.

8. Things that are made of glass in your classroom.

9. Things that would live in a small cage.

10. Things that make music.

11. Things that feel wet.

12. Things that have numbers on them.

13. Things that have letters on them.

14. Things you can ride on.

15. Things that are chewy.

IV-3   TELL ME ABOUT IT!

Objective: The student will relate information meaningfully to others by describing objects.

Directions

To the teacher: This page is intended to initiate discussion among the students about how to describe objects. The student should be alerted to the fact that there are different ways to describe something—the *color* of it (for example, a skunk's color is pretty descriptive), its *shape* or *size* (for example, the roundness of a ball is inherent to its being a ball), *function* (the purpose of an umbrella is to keep the rain off someone), *location* (one might look for car keys in a purse if that is where they are usually kept), *who* might use it (a baby would be the likely recipient of a bottle or rattle), or what it *feels* like (the flame of a candle would be pretty hot). Students should try to think of things that might best be described primarily by their color, their function, and so on.

To the student: We are going to talk about different ways to describe objects. This page gives some examples of how we might tell about something. Think about why the picture clue is a good example. For instance, why do people usually describe skunks as "black and white?" (after mention is made of the smell, of course!) **(Answer:** It's one of the most obvious characteristics of a skunk.) Why do we describe a ball as round? **(Answer:** A ball is something that can roll, and to do that it has to be round.) Continue discussion of the other ways to describe objects. Ask students if they can come up with other ways to tell about something.

TELL ME ABOUT IT!

You can describe a thing in several ways:

COLOR...

SHAPE or SIZE...

what it DOES...

where you would FIND it...

who would USE it...

 or what it FEELS like.

Can you think of other ways to tell about something?

IV-4 RIZBO IS BACK!

Objective: The student will relate information meaningfully to others by describing objects.

Directions

To the teacher: The situation on this worksheet is that Rizbo, the creature from the planet Uggot, needs another English lesson. He is having trouble describing objects that he encountered on his vacation to earth, and requests help from the students to describe them. Students, either singly or in small groups, can try to come up with descriptions of common objects. This activity could be done orally or in writing.

To the student: I want you to help Rizbo describe the objects on the page. Remember to use helpful words like the kinds of words we talked about before (examples: the color of the object, its shape, and so on).

Answers

Typical responses may include:

1. desk—hard, brown, use it to write on, find it at school
2. pencil—long, thin, yellow, has a point, use it to write
3. shoe—brown, wear it on your feet, comes in pairs, used by people
4. book—square, use it to find information, find it at school
5. sandwich—square, soft, white, eat it
6. basketball—orangish, round, find it in a gym, used by people
7. record player—square, used to play records, find it at school
8. pencil sharpener—hangs on a wall, used to sharpen pencils

NAME _____   DATE _____

RIZBO IS BACK!

Rizbo is still having trouble describing what things were like on earth. Can you help him tell about these things? (Remember the helpful ways to describe things?)

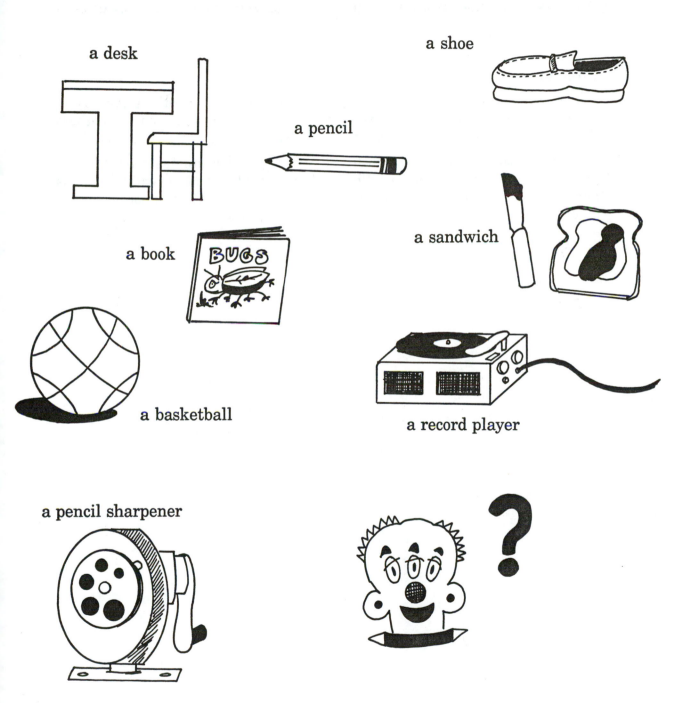

a desk

a shoe

a pencil

a book

a sandwich

a basketball

a record player

a pencil sharpener

IV-5 WHAT'S IN THE BAG?

Objective: The student will relate information meaningfully to others by describing objects.

Directions

To the teacher: The students will draw a picture of something they could put into a bag (for example, a small object). Then they will give clues to others that would help them guess what their object is.

To the student: I want you to draw a picture of something that would fit in a bag. Don't tell anyone what it is! When everyone has finished, we will take turns giving clues (remember the describing words we've been talking about?) so that others can try to guess what's in our bag.

WHAT'S IN THE BAG?

Pretend you brought something to school today in a brown bag. You can draw a picture of it if you want to. Then think of some clues to tell others in the class so they can guess what is in your bag. Don't make it too easy!

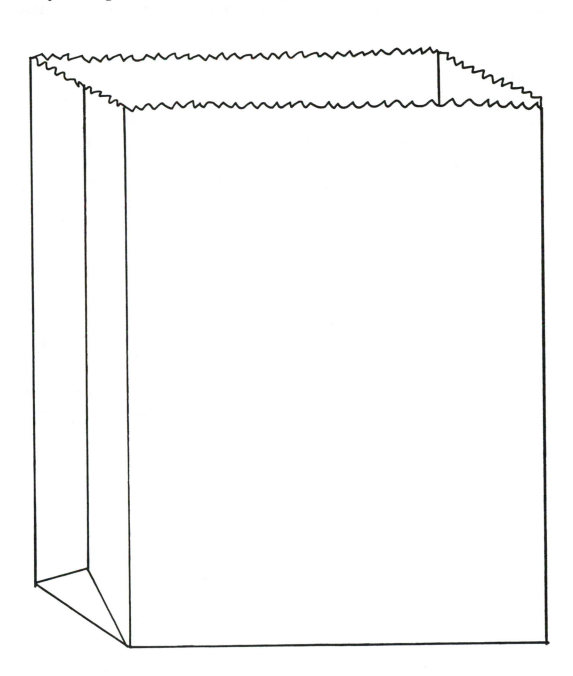

IV-6 FACTS AND OPINIONS

Objective: The student will relate information meaningfully to others by stating facts and opinions.

Directions

To the teacher: This page introduces *facts* and *opinions* and some differences between the two. Suggest that if students think of a *fact* in terms of "I know...(something to be true), and an *opinion* as "I think...(something is true), they may help make a distinction. Discuss the examples with the students.

To the student: We are going to learn about facts and opinions. A *fact* is something that is always true (give examples). An *opinion* is something that might be true, but someone else might not think it's true (give examples). Let's talk about some of the facts and opinions on this sheet.

Answers (to discussion)

1. Facts: A black cat is always black, everyone agrees on what *black* is. If you live in a house, you live in a house! The TV can be either on or off, not in between. The day of the week is not debatable—it's run by the clock.
2. Opinions: Someone may not like the same pizza that you like; someone may think that pizza isn't good at all. Some people don't like to jump rope (they may not be good at it); others think it's fun.

NAME _____   DATE _____

FACTS AND OPINIONS

1. A FACT is what is always *true* about something. Say: "I know..."

That is a black cat!

I live in a house.

The TV is on.

Today is Monday.

2. An OPINION is what you *think* about something...but it might not be what everyone else thinks!
   Say: "I think..."

IV-7   DO DOGS HAVE FOUR LEGS?

Objective: The student will relate information meaningfully to others by stating facts and opinions.

Directions

To the teacher: Students will read or listen to a statement and decide whether or not it is a fact—something that is always true—or an opinion-something that is just what they think about it. At this point, students may need clarification on the overlap between facts and opinions. Their opinion may also be a fact. ("I think that dog is a collie" may turn out to be a fact if the dog is, indeed a cousin of Lassie.) Another point of clarification is that an opinion may be just as important as a fact. Saying that it is "just their opinion" doesn't necessarily mean that it isn't important!

To the student: On this sheet, you are going to read/listen to some statements and try to decide whether they are facts or opinions. You are going to circle the answer (fact or opinion) on the sheet. Remember to think about whether the statement is always true, or if it's what someone thinks about it at the time.

Answers

1. opinion
2. opinion
3. fact
4. fact
5. opinion—someone else might think a C is awful!
6. fact
7. opinion—someone might not enjoy singing at all.
8. fact (dogs who have been injured do not count!)
9. opinion

DO DOGS HAVE FOUR LEGS?

Is each statement a *fact* or an *opinion*?
Is it what is always true (a fact) or what *you* think about something (opinion)? Circle your answer.

1. This hot dog needs more ketchup!

      FACT   OPINION

2. This hot dog is too hot!

      FACT   OPINION

3. My reading book has a star on it.

      FACT   OPINION

4. My pencil is broken.

      FACT   OPINION

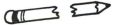

5. I did a great job on this spelling test!

      FACT   OPINION

6. I got a B+ on my math paper.

      FACT   OPINION

7. Singing is fun!

      FACT   OPINION

8. A dog has four legs.

      FACT   OPINION

9. Pizza is the best food.

      FACT   OPINION

IV-8 JUST THE FACTS!

Objective: The student will relate information meaningfully to others by stating facts and opinions.

Directions

To the teacher: This is an oral activity. Students are to think of facts about the objects on the worksheet. Encourage students to think of several facts for each object. Discuss why they are facts, not opinions.

To the student: On this sheet, I want you to tell a fact (remember what that is?) about each object pictured. Listen to others tell their facts and see if we can pick out which ones are facts, not opinions.

Answers

Answers will vary, but typical facts may include:

1. bus–a bus has wheels
2. hamburgers–hamburgers are made of meat (we hope!)
3. your foot–is at the end of your leg
4. a book–has pages
5. your eyes–open and close
6. baseball–is a game
7. your school–is on _____ street ("...is yucky" is an opinion)
8. a football–is used in a game
9. a computer–is a machine
10. water fountains–spray water
11. milk cartons–are made of cardboard (or plastic)

JUST THE FACTS!

Tell a FACT (it is always true) about:

1. a bus

2. hamburgers

3. your foot

4. a book

5. your eyes

6. baseball

7. your school

8. a football

9. a computer

10. water fountains

11. milk cartons

IV-9   WHAT'S YOUR OPINION?

Objective: The student will relate information meaningfully by stating facts and opinions.

Directions

To the teacher: This activity can be performed orally. Students are to think of opinions about the objects on the worksheet. Ask several students to give opinions so all will realize that everyone doesn't necessarily feel the same way about something, but that everyone is entitled to his or her opinion. There is no right or wrong on this.

To the student: On this sheet, I want you to think about your opinion on the objects you see pictured. I will ask several people to give their opinions about the object, and I'll bet not all of them will be the same. Why is that? (People are individuals and have different likes and dislikes.)

Answers

Answers will vary, but typical opinions may include:

1. spaghetti– is hot, spicy, delicious
2. your sister–is ugly
3. dogs–are playful
4. the playground–is too crowded
5. school–is okay
6. your best friend–is someone who shares toys
7. homework–takes up too much time
8. chocolate–is expensive
9. rain–is fun
10. football–is a boring game
11. peanut butter–tastes like peanuts

WHAT'S YOUR OPINION?

Tell your OPINION (what you think) about:

1. spaghetti

2. your sister

3. dogs

4. the playground

5. school

6. your best friend

7. homework

8. chocolate

9. rain

10. football

11. peanut butter

IV-10 TELL ME MORE

Objective: The student will relate information meaningfully by explaining while answering questions.

Directions

To the teacher: Sometimes children need to give a bit more information to fully explain their answers to questions. The worksheet gives examples of situations in which a simple one-word answer isn't enough to help the person understand the problem. The students are to think of what the children on the worksheet could say in order to "tell more" about their answer or problem.

To the student: The children on this sheet are answering questions, but they need to tell the teacher more to get the help they need. The teacher can't read the children's minds, so they have to be better at explaining what the teacher needs to know. See if you can think of what else the child in each story could say that would give more information.

Answers (examples)

1. "The bracelet is red, with a gold clasp, it's long, and I left it on top of my desk before we went to recess."
2. "I can't get the numbers to add up right. I keep coming up with two more than the answer book has in it."
3. "We were playing baseball during recess, and Tommy hit the ball a little too hard and it crashed through the window. But we got a home run!"

TELL ME MORE

1. Sally is missing her bracelet. She thinks she lost it somewhere in the classroom.

What else could Sally say?

2. David is having trouble on his math paper.

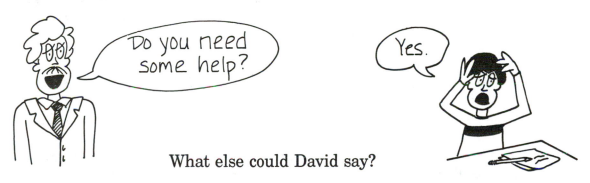

What else could David say?

3. Some children were playing on the playground with a baseball. Look what happened!

How could they tell more?

IV-11   TELL ME EVEN MORE!

Objective: The student will relate information meaningfully to others by explaining while answering questions.

Directions

To the teacher: This worksheet is similar to the previous one, in that the student must answer the question by telling a few sentences of explanation.

To the student: Today we are going to work some more on explaining your answers. There are 10 questions to answer. Think about how you could give a complete answer using several sentences. I will call on several students to answer these questions, so listen for good explanations.

Answers

Typical answers may include:

1. Turn on Highway 37, go north for 2 miles, and there it is! Make sure you look for a white house with green shutters.
2. I go into the coatroom and look for an empty hook. Then I put my mittens in the pockets and put my coat on the hook.
3. I wait outside my house until the bus comes. Then I transfer to another bus at the high school. Then I ride that bus to this school.
4. Last night my mom and I went to a movie. After the movie, we had pizza at the Italian restaurant. After that, we went home.
5. This weekend I am going to a birthday party for my cousin. We are going to the store to buy her a doll for a gift.
6. My sister is pretty nice. She's funny, and laughs a lot. She's short.
7. First I read it. Then I took it home. Then my sister read it.
8. I watched a movie about cowboys. Then I watched the news.
9. My dog was in the hospital for awhile. She was hit by a car and broke her tail. The vet says she'll be all right.
10. Our team won the football game. The score was 10–7 and it was great!

TELL ME EVEN MORE!

1. How do you get to your house?

2. Where do you put your coat when you come in?

3. How did you come to school today?

4. What did you do last night?

5. What are you going to do this weekend?

6. What is your sister like?

7. What did you do with your library book?

8. What did you watch on TV last night?

9. How is your dog?

10. Who won the football game?

IV-12 HOW DO YOU CHEW GUM?

Objective: The student will relate information meaningfully to others by explaining while answering questions.

Directions

To the teacher: The students are going to explain how to do simple day-to-day activities as if they were explaining them to someone who has no prior knowledge of how to perform the activity. Rizbo, the space creature, is the "person" who wants to know how to do something. By giving him directions, the student must explain things carefully, logically, and fairly simply. You may wish to have the students work in small groups so that they can polish their instructions and come up with one that is the best and most clear.

To the student: Rizbo, our space friend, needs to learn how to do a few earth activities that you know how to do without even thinking about it. But now I want you to think about it. How would you explain to him how to do these easy things? It's harder than you would think!

Answers

Answers will vary, but look for clear directions, logical sequencing of steps, and no omissions of crucial steps! (for example, taking off the wrapping paper on a piece of gum, or, putting the shoe on your foot, or getting the ball out of the closet!)

HOW DO YOU CHEW GUM?

Rizbo is trying to understand some things that earth people do. He has never heard of these things before! Try to explain to him how to:

chew gum

eat a banana

roller skate

put on a coat

tie a shoe

sharpen a pencil

eat lunch in the cafeteria

play dodgeball

walk backwards

Re: Describing past, present, and created events

Dear Parents,

We are continuing our oral language lessons on everyday talking skills—in particular, *obtaining and exchanging information with others*. We will now be concentrating on *describing events* to others—that we do daily and things we already did—and creating stories about pictures.

At home, you can extend these activities by asking the age-old parent-child question: What did you do at school today? *Look* for some answers, because we'll be working at school on *having something to say!*

At times, we may be talking about good (or just plain vivid) memories of *past experiences.* Your child might ask for old photographs, souvenirs of a good vacation, or your recollections of details about what happened that summer when he or she went to camp.

Finally, having your child *tell you stories from pictures* can be an activity first accomplished by using familiar storybooks. Cover the text, concentrate on the pictures, and have him or her retell the story. You can also look for interesting pictures in old magazines or photo albums and send them to school. You may get a copy of some great stories written or told about them!

Sincerely,

_____

Teacher

IV-13   THE NEW STUDENT

Objective: The student will relate information meaningfully to others by talking about daily activities with peers and teachers.

Directions

To the teacher: The students are going to pretend they are explaining their daily activities to a new student who has just joined the class. The new student has posed a question, and others need to answer her questions so that she will understand what to do and how to do it. The students can probably compile lists or a sequence of activities to present to this new student to assist her in adjusting to the class. Try to emphasize logical sequencing, clear explanations, and meaningful information.

To the student: You are going to pretend that a new student has joined our class. She needs to learn how to do a lot of things before she will feel comfortable in the class. Here are her questions; now let's see if you can work together to come up with the best way to answer them. Tell her what she needs to know in the right order and very clearly.

Answers

Typical responses may include the following items, but should be longer:

1. Bookbag, pencil, ruler.
2. Reading book, spelling book, math workbook.
3. First, we talk about current events.
4. Buy a lunch ticket or bring lunch from home.
5. Recess, science, social studies.
6. Through the door on Main Street.
7. No, the teacher will assign you a seat.
8. The janitor will raise the desk for you.
9. At the school store on Thursdays.
10. Gym shoes.
11. Next to the principal's office.
12. There's a lost-and-found box in the office.

THE NEW STUDENT

Linda is a new student in your classroom. She needs to know a lot of things about your school and your classroom. Can you help her?

1. What do I need to bring to school?

2. What books do you use?

3. What do you do first?

4. What do I do about lunch?

5. What do you do in the afternoon?

6. Where do we enter the building?

7. Can I sit anywhere in the room?

8. What if my desk is too low?

9. Where can I buy paper?

10. What do I need for P.E.?

11. Where is the school nurse?

12. What do I do if I can't find my mitten?

IV-14 WHAT DID YOU DO TODAY?

Objective: The student will relate information meaningfully to others by talking about daily activities with peers and teachers.

Directions

To the teacher: One way to talk about daily activities is (a) to summarize with the students the events of the day, (b) to further discuss why the activities were included, and (c) how the students did on them. An optional extension (d) involves speculation of how the activities could have been improved. For example, a class chart could be compiled (a) listing or stating the activity (WHAT did we do?), (b) suggesting reasons for engaging in the activity (WHY did we do it?), (c) evaluating the activity (HOW did we do on it?), and optional activity (d) extending the activity to include modifications of the activity (NEXT TIME we'll......). The class chart could be drawn on the chalkboard, or students may make their own charts and then compile the information.

To the student: A lot of times you go home and your parents ask you, "What did you do today?" and you say, "Nothing." Well, today we're going to take a look at what we usually do during the day and think about why we do it; how we're doing on it, and what could make it even better. Then when you go home, you'll have lots of things to tell your parents about! Think about *why* we do these things, as well as *what* we do.

Answers

A typical chart may resemble the following:

WHAT did we do?	WHY did we do it?	HOW did we do?	NEXT TIME we'll
1. current events	so we'll know what's going on in the world and community	not very well— no one brought in pictures from the paper	remember to bring in newspaper pictures
2. Flash cards for math	so we'll learn multiplication	pretty well— everyone knew them	do division flashcards

208

WHAT DID YOU DO TODAY?

WHAT did we do?	WHY did we do it?	HOW did we do?	NEXT TIME we'll

IV-15 ONE TIME I...

Objective: The student will relate information meaningfully to others by describing past experiences.

Directions

To the teacher: This worksheet is intended to conjure up some past experiences that the child may have had so that he or she can talk about them. Explain that everyone has had different experiences with the same event (for example, Christmas). It's interesting to hear about how other people have had good, bad, interesting, funny, or crazy things happen to them. Call on several students to relate their experiences for the entire class, and then try to summarize the experience. Was it a good experience? Fun? Why? You may wish to compile a list of "feeling" words on the board for children to draw from and add to.

To the student: Today we are going to talk about things that have already happened—the past. Maybe these things happened a long time ago, or maybe they happened just a little while ago. But they already happened and are now *over.* We are going to listen to some of you tell us about some of these experiences you may have had, and then try to decide whether your experience was a good experience, a bad one, a funny or crazy experience, or just what kind of feeling it gave you.

Answers

Answers will vary.

ONE TIME I...

had fun in the snow

went on a vacation with my family

got a new pet

had a birthday party

made a big mistake

played a trick on someone else

laughed very hard

did something scary

played with a new toy

had a great Christmas

learned something interesting

got hurt

did something dumb

went to the hospital

made someone feel very happy

visited my grandmother

swam in the ocean

was very proud of myself

IV-16   ON THE PLAYGROUND

Objective: The student will relate information meaningfully to others by creating short stories about pictures.

Directions

To the teacher: The students will look at a picture of children playing on a playground. Using this as a stimulus, they can either tell or write short stories about some event or events that they see in the picture. Students can relate their stories to the whole class.

To the student: You are going to look at a picture of some children playing on a playground. There are a lot of things going on, aren't there? I want you to look carefully around this picture and see if you can make up a short story about something that's going on in it. Then we'll hear some of your stories and see if they fit the picture.

Answers

The stories will vary, but look for meaningfulness in the stories. Creativity is welcomed; of course, you do want the story to fit with the events depicted on the worksheet.

NAME _____   DATE _____

ON THE PLAYGROUND

IV-17   IN THE CLASSROOM

Objective: The student will relate information meaningfully to others by creating short stories about pictures.

Directions

To the teacher: The setting on this worksheet is the classroom. Students are to look at the activities going on in the room and create (by writing or telling) short stories about the picture. Have students share their stories with the class.

To the student: You are going to see a picture of children in a classroom. Look very carefully at the things going on in the room, and see if you can make up a short story about something you see. We'll tell our stories when everyone is finished.

Answers

Stories will vary.

IN THE CLASSROOM

IV-18   ON THE BUS

Objective: The student will relate information meaningfully to others by creating short stories about pictures.

Directions

To the teacher: The students will look at a picture of children riding on a school bus. They will create short stories about what they see happening on the bus and write or tell about their stories.

To the student: This picture shows children riding on a school bus. What do you think is happening? I want you to make up a story about something you see in the picture. We'll share our stories when everyone is finished.

Answers

Stories will vary.

ON THE BUS

IV-19   IN THE OFFICE

Objective: The student will relate information meaningfully to others by creating short stories about pictures.

Directions

To the teacher: The students will look at a picture of a typical school office, with principal's office, nurse's room, secretary in back of a typewriter, and various and assorted children in the office area. The student is to create a short story, written or oral, about some event in the picture.

To the student: Today you are going to see a picture of the school office in an ordinary school. Do you think it looks like ours? I want you to look carefully around the picture and pick out something you see in the picture that you would like to make a short story about. We'll hear your stories when everyone's finished. Remember to make your story fit the picture

Answers

Stories will vary.

IN THE OFFICE

Re: Using appropriate oral communication

Dear Parents,

    Our final activities in everyday talking skills deal with *appropriateness* in talking to others. Not only does what you say have to make sense, but *timing* is important too. How many times have you found yourself scolding your child, "NOT NOW—can't you see I'm BUSY?" Take a moment—then—to help him understand why the question is OK, but the situation or setting isn't.

    We will be talking about *emotions or feelings*. Help your child identify her feelings from time to time (for example, I'll bet that homerun made you feel happy! You look kind of sad; anything wrong?).

    A final skill for which your help is truly desired is that of practicing the *polite greetings and partings* we'll be learning at school. A cheerful "Bye, Mom," or "Good morning, Dad," can start and end a day on a much nicer note. Prepare your child with a friendly comment for the bus driver. And—be a good model yourself! You're his other teacher!

Sincerely,

_____

Teacher

IV-20 NANCY'S PROBLEM

Objective: The student will obtain information by asking the following types of questions at appropriate times to appropriate people: who, whose, what, when where?

Directions

To the teacher: The situation on this worksheet is that a child has a problem (she cannot find her bookbag). The student is to help the child solve her problem by obtaining information. The questions on the worksheet are intended to help the student decide how the child should go about solving her problem and what circumstances are the best for obtaining information.

To the student: Nancy is a child with a problem—she is missing something. We're going to try to help Nancy solve her problem by asking questions to get the information she needs. We'll talk about people she could ask for help, and then we'll talk about when would be a good time to talk to those people. There may be lots of good answers, so tell us what you think! What should Nancy do? Why?

Answers

Answers will vary according to the personnel available in the school, the rules or procedures that exist in the school and classroom, and how the child perceives the situation. For example, the janitor may be an excellent resource person if the janitor in your school cleans out the coat room in every classroom every day after school. Before school may be a bad time to talk to the principal if that is when he or she has parent conferences. The children will have to think about their choices and explain why it would or would not work in their situation.

NANCY'S PROBLEM

Nancy cannot find her bookbag. She thought she left it in the coat room, but it's not there. Let's help Nancy with her problem.

1. What does she need to know?

2. Whom should she ask to find out?

   her teacher?

   the janitor?

   her mother?

   a friend in her class?

   someone who came in at the same time she did?

   the principal?

   another teacher?

   the school nurse?

   the secretary?

3. When is a good time to ask?

   before school?

   after school?

   during a fire drill?

   during her reading group?

   during someone else's reading group?

   during lunch?

   during recess?

   when she is on the bus?

IV-21 MORE PROBLEMS

Objective: The student will obtain information by asking the following types of questions at appropriate times to appropriate people: who, whose, what, when, where?

Directions

To the teacher: Students will continue to think about asking questions at appropriate times of appropriate people in order to help solve problems. The worksheet may be completed orally or in writing.

To the student: Today you are going to help three more children ask questions to solve their problems. Remember to think about what question they need to ask, of whom they should ask the question, and when would be a good time to ask it.

Answers

Answers may vary, but typical responses may include:

Donald
1. "What word is that?" 2. The teacher (she was walking around the room, not occupied) 3. Ask the teacher when she comes to his side of the room.

Amy
1. "What are we having for lunch today?" 2. The teacher, if she's agreeable to being interrupted when she's doing her lunch count; otherwise, a fellow student perhaps? 3. Ask the teacher when she has finished the lunch count, or ask another student before she sits down at her desk.

Scott
1. "What was our spelling assignment?" 2. Another student, the teacher. 3. Before he gets on the bus, or on the bus if another classmate who knows the assignment rides with him.

MORE PROBLEMS

Help these children find out what they need to know. These questions may help you:

      1. What question do they need to ask?

      2. Whom should they ask?

      3. When should they ask it?

Donald is reading a library book. He came to a long word that he didn't know. His teacher was walking around the room.

      1. What question? _____

      2. Whom? _____

      3. When? _____

Amy wants to know what they are having for lunch today. She just got off the bus and walked into her classroom. Her teacher is taking the lunch count.

      1. What question? _____

      2. Whom? _____

      3. When? _____

Scott forgot to copy down his homework assignment for spelling. The buses are just about ready to come. The class is getting ready to leave.

      1. What question? _____

      2. Whom? _____

      3. When? _____

IV-22 STILL MORE PROBLEMS

Objective: The student will obtain information by asking the following types of questions at appropriate times of appropriate people: who, whose, what, when, where?

Directions

To the teacher: Eight additional problem situations are presented to the students for practice in using questions to obtain information at appropriate times from appropriate people. Students can work on these problems individually, in small groups, or as a class.

To the student: Here are some more problems that children have. See if you can help them ask good questions at good times to solve their problems by finding out what they need to know.

Answers

Answers will vary.

STILL MORE PROBLEMS

1. Louis can't find his math book. It is almost time for math class to start. He thought he left it in his desk, but it's not there. The teacher is getting ready to start the math lesson.

2. Amanda's teacher asked her to go to the art supply room to get some cans of paint for the class. She got to the art room, but no one was in it. She saw another teacher walking down the hall.

3. Michael's class is ready to start their spelling lesson. Michael let Ronny use his spelling book yesterday, but Ronny didn't give it back. Ronny sits on the other side of the room.

4. The buses are not going to park in front of the school today, because the workers are painting the lines in the parking lot. Sandy doesn't know where she is supposed to get on the bus.

5. Jennifer wants to know whose turn it is to change the calendar. The teacher is getting the class lined up to go to recess.

6. Ken is looking through a book during silent reading time. He comes to a picture of a very strange animal and wants to know what it is. The teacher is sitting at her desk, grading papers.

7. Glenn found a blue mitten outside during recess. He brought it back into the classroom with him. The students in the class are coming back from recess and getting in their seats.

8. Alice is getting <u>very</u> hungry. She looked at the clock, but doesn't know how close it is to lunch time. Then the fire drill bell goes off.

IV-23 MAY I?

Objective: The student will obtain information by asking the following types of questions at appropriate times of appropriate people: could, may, can, are, does, should?

Directions

To the teacher: This page provides practice for the student in asking questions involving permission, assistance, or other information. The questions may start with words like: Can I? May I? Do I? There may be several ways to ask the same question. You want to stress that this time instead of answering questions, they will be asking questions. Asking questions clearly is as important as answering them correctly.

To the student: You are going to pretend you are in a situation where you have to ask someone a question in order to know if you have permission to do something, or if you need some help with something, or if you need to know something more. I want you to think about a good question that you could ask to get the information you need.

Answers

Typical responses may include:

1. May I wash the chalkboard?
2. Do you want me to take these boots off?
3. Could we do our reading first?
4. May we use markers on our spelling test?
5. Could I call my mother?
6. May I borrow that pencil?
7. Please may I be excused?
8. Can you get that book for me?
9. Are you going to the basketball game?
10. Should we add on this page or subtract?
11. Could I go to the office?
12. Could you tell me what that word is?
13. Should I go back on the bus and get my homework?
14. Is it time for my medication?
15. Do you have any new stickers I could use?

MAY I?

How could you ask a question for each of the following situations?

1. You want to know if you may wash the chalkboard.

2. You want to know if the teacher wants you to take off your muddy boots.

3. You want to do your reading group first today, instead of second.

4. You want to use markers instead of a pencil on your spelling test.

5. You want to call your mother from the office.

6. You want to borrow a pencil from your friend who sits next to you.

7. You want to know if you can be excused to go to the restroom.

8. You want someone to get a book for you that is out of your reach.

9. You want to know if your friend is going to the basketball game after school.

10. You want to know whether you should add or subtract on your math page.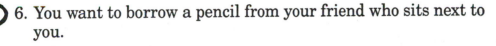

11. Your stomach hurts and you want to go to the office.

12. You are reading and come to a word you don't know.

13. You left your homework on the bus and want to know if you can go back and get it.

14. You want to know if it is time for your medication.

15. You want to know if your teacher has any new stickers.

IV-24   DOES IT?

Objective: The student will obtain information by asking the following types of questions at appropriate times of appropriate people: could, can, are, does, should?

Directions

To the teacher: This is a continuation of the situations on the previous worksheet. The student is to ask an appropriate question that would enable him or her to obtain the information needed in the situations. This could be done orally or in writing (to compare the different ways of asking a question to obtain the same information).

To the student: Here are some more situations in which you will pretend you need to get some information from someone by asking a question. Think about the different questions you could ask to get the same information.

Answers

Typical responses may include:

1. Do you have my homework assignment ready?
2. Do you think the flowers need to be watered?
3. Will there be school tomorrow?
4. Did you borrow my gym shoes?
5. Does the gerbil need some food?
6. Do you need any help with that bulletin board?
7. Would you like us to pass the papers forward?
8. Are we supposed to put our chairs up?
9. Do you want us to bring a pencil?
10. Do we have computer class on Wednesdays or on Thursdays?
11. Is our group supposed to be out in the hall or at the table?
12. Do report cards go home in the mail or in our hands?
13. Do the hamburgers have ketchup on them?

DOES IT?

How could you ask a question for each of the following situations?

1. You want to know if your teacher has your homework assignment ready.

2. You want to know if the flowers need more water.

3. You want to know if there will be school tomorrow.

4. You want to know if your friend borrowed your gym shoes.

5. You want to know if the gerbil needs more food.

6. You want to know if the art teacher needs any help putting up the bulletin board.

7. You want to know if the teacher wants you all to pass your papers up to the front.

8. You want to know if you are supposed to put up your chairs on top of your desks at the end of the day.

9. You want to know if the teacher wants you to bring a pencil to reading group.

10. You want to know if you have computer class on Wednesdays or Thursdays.

11. You want to know if your group is supposed to work out in the hall or at the table in the back.

12. You want to know if report cards will go home by mail or in your hand.

13. You want to know if the hamburgers at the cafeteria have ketchup on them.

IV-25   HOW I FEEL TODAY

Objective: The student will express emotions verbally to peers and adults.

Directions

To the teacher: This is an introductory page to discuss emotions—what "emotions" means, what some emotions are, and the conditions under which we might feel certain emotions.

To the student: We are going to be talking about emotions for awhile. "Emotions" is a big word, but simply means how you feel. Look at the first picture. That boy is *happy*. What are some reasons you can think of that he might be happy? (got a good grade, got a birthday present). How can you tell he's happy? (smiling, looks excited).

Look at the second picture. That girl is *sad*. Why do you think she might be sad? (goldfish died, hurt her finger). How could you tell she was sad? (eyes down, tears).

Look at the third picture. That boy is *confused*. Does anybody know what that means? (mixed up, not sure what to do). What might he be confused about? (not understanding something, didn't know what to do). How could you tell he was confused? (hands out, puzzled look on face).

Look at the last picture. That boy is *angry*. Why do you think he might be angry? (someone kicked him, tore up his book). How could you tell me was angry? (red face, frowning mouth, shaking fists).

How do *you* feel right now? (Allow time for students to respond.)

Why? (Allow time for discussion.)

Sometimes we don't have reasons why we feel a certain way; we just feel happy, or in a bad mood. But it helps to think about what mood we're in, what emotion we're feeling at the moment. It might help others understand us better, and help us to understand ourselves better too.

HOW I FEEL TODAY

Emotions are like feelings.
You might feel

HAPPY...

SAD...

CONFUSED...

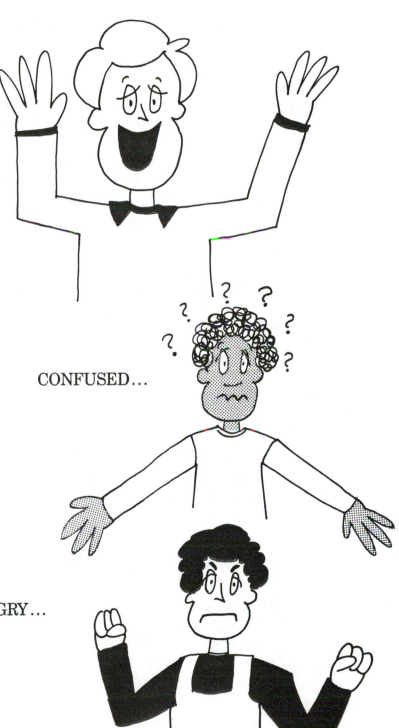

ANGRY...

**How do you feel right now?
Why?**

IV-26 HOW WOULD YOU FEEL IF...

Objective: The student will express emotions verbally to peers and adults.

Directions

To the teacher: The students will read or listen to 10 statements that describe a situation. They are to think about how it would make a person (in general) feel. They are to draw a smile, frown, question mark, or exclamation mark on the face to depict how they think someone would feel. This activity could also be done orally if it is confusing to the students to draw the facial expressions.

To the student: We are going to do some more thinking about how situations make you feel—happy, sad, confused, or angry. There are other emotions or feelings, but we are just going to think about those four for now. As we read each of the 10 situations, think about how it would make someone feel. If it would make you happy, you will draw a smile on the face; if it would make you feel sad, draw a frown on the face; if it would make you feel mixed up or confused, draw a question mark on the face; and if it would make you feel angry, draw an exclamation mark on the face. (Demonstrate, or call attention to examples of these marks on the worksheet.)

Answers

There may be some variance of opinion. If the student can justify a response, you may consider it correct if it is appropriate.

1. happy
2. angry
3. confused
4. angry
5. sad (angry? confused?)
6. confused
7. happy
8. sad
9. confused
10. angry

HOW WOULD YOU FEEL IF...

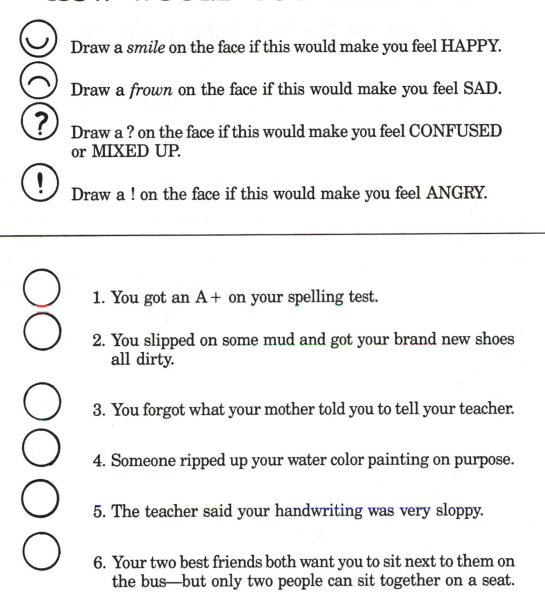

Draw a *smile* on the face if this would make you feel HAPPY.

Draw a *frown* on the face if this would make you feel SAD.

Draw a ? on the face if this would make you feel CONFUSED or MIXED UP.

Draw a ! on the face if this would make you feel ANGRY.

---

1. You got an A+ on your spelling test.

2. You slipped on some mud and got your brand new shoes all dirty.

3. You forgot what your mother told you to tell your teacher.

4. Someone ripped up your water color painting on purpose.

5. The teacher said your handwriting was very sloppy.

6. Your two best friends both want you to sit next to them on the bus—but only two people can sit together on a seat.

7. A friend gave you some smelly stickers that you have wanted for a long time.

8. No one picked you to be on one of the teams for kickball.

9. You couldn't hear what the teacher said to do in your workbook and then he said, "Get started right now."

10. Someone poked you in the back as he walked past your desk.

IV-27　WHAT WOULD YOU SAY?

Objective: The student will express emotions verbally to peers and adults.

Directions

To the teacher: This page presents situations in which the student would probably feel a certain way (happy, sad, and so forth). The student is to tell what he or she would say to convey this feeling to someone else.

To the student: We are going to look at different ways to let other people know how you feel by telling them. In each situation, I want you to think first about how it would make you feel, and then think of a way that you would tell someone how you feel. There might be several ways to say similar things, so listen while I call on people to answer.

Answers

Typical examples may include:

1. Happy–I am so proud of myself.
2. Sad–I didn't like it when you said that.
3. Confused–I didn't know how to read any of the words. I felt as if I had somebody else's book.
4. Angry–I don't like to have spitballs thrown at me!
5. Happy–I feel very smart!
6. Sad–I feel awful.
7. Confused–I don't know what I'm doing wrong.
8. Sad–I feel as if everyone is laughing at me.
9. Happy–I love recess! I can't wait to play on the swings!
10. Sad–All I can think is that she might die.
11. Confused–I don't know which table I'm supposed to be at.
12. Happy–I picked this out myself.
13. Confused–I don't know where the food is.

WHAT WOULD YOU SAY?

What would you say to let someone know how you feel IF...

1. the teacher said you had the best book report in the whole class?

2. your friend said you were fat?

3. you couldn't read any of the words in your reading book?

4. someone threw a spitball at you at lunch?

5. you won the spelling bee?

6. you got an F on your math test?

7. you kept adding the same numbers together but never got the right answer?

8. you dropped your tray full of food in the lunchroom?

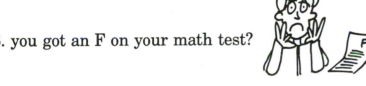

9. the teacher gave your class extra recess time?

10. you are thinking about your sick dog?

11. your teacher said to sit at the big table in back of the room, but both of the tables are big?

12. your friend said she likes your new sweatshirt?

13. it is your turn to feed the fish but you can't find the fish food anywhere?

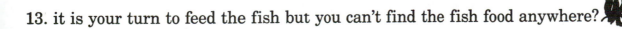

IV-28 GREETING THE BUS DRIVER

Objective: The student will greet others appropriately.

Directions

To the teacher: One of the first people many students will meet in their school day is the bus driver. Good greetings can be practiced the moment they step on the bus. This workshseet is designed to have the student identify polite ways to greet the bus driver. Students can discuss the situations orally and indicate polite greetings by circling the polite students and/or putting an X on the impolite students. You may wish to discuss ways they have observed students on their bus greeting the bus driver and whether or not these greetings are polite.

To the student: For awhile, we will be discussing ways to meet or greet people, and ways to say goodbye when you leave someone. It's important to be polite when you are with other people, and this is one way that you can practice every day—by greeting your bus driver. On this sheet, we are going to look at six different children and six different bus drivers. Some of the children are not very polite. Let's see if you can find the ones who are polite when they greet the bus driver and put a circle around them. Think about why they are polite and why the impolite students are not being as nice as they could be.

Answers

1. Polite–greeting, called bus driver by name
2. Impolite–didn't acknowledge bus driver, has immediate complaint
3. Impolite–is saying "hi," but has an angry face as if he doesn't really mean to be friendly
4. Polite–greets and waves
5. Impolite–has an immediate complaint, didn't greet bus driver
6. Polite–polite greeting, smiling

GREETING THE BUS DRIVER

IV-29   GREETING THE TEACHER

Objective: The student will greet others appropriately.

Directions

To the teacher: Another person who deserves to be greeted in the school day is the teacher! On this sheet, a situation is depicted in which children are entering a classroom and their comments to the teacher are written by the children. Students are to read or listen to the comments and decide whether they are polite greetings to the teacher and discuss why. You may wish to have the students circle the polite children and put an X on the children who are not polite.

To the student: On this sheet, we see children coming into a classroom. Who is someone they could be greeting in this picture. (teacher)? Next to each child entering the classroom is a balloon telling what that child is saying to the teacher. I want you to think about whether that child is greeting the teacher in a nice way. If so, put a circle around him or her. If the child isn't greeting the teacher in a nice way, put an X on the child. Maybe we can help those children think of nice ways to greet their teacher.

Answers

1. polite
2. impolite
3. impolite
4. polite
5. polite
6. impolite
7. impolite
8. polite
9. polite

GREETING THE TEACHER

IV-30   GREETING PEERS

Objective: The student will greet others appropriately.

Directions

To the teacher: Students can practice their greeting skills with peers as they enter the classroom each day. This page shows the beginning of a class day, as children enter and find their desks. Some of the children are greeting each other politely and some are not. The students are to indicate the polite children by circling them, and indicate the impolite children by putting an X on them. Discuss ways that are polite to greet others and why some ways are not as good. (For example, silence is not necessarily impolite, but it's not actively polite either!)

To the student: You are going to look at a picture of children entering a classroom. The children are saying things to each other. Some of them are greeting each other politely by saying nice things; others are not greeting each other with nice things. I want you to find the children who are polite and circle them; put an X on the children who are not saying polite things to greet others.

Answers

1. polite (initiated greeting)
2. polite (reciprocated greeting)
3. impolite
4. impolite (reciprocated impoliteness)
5. polite
6. impolite
7. polite
8. polite
9. polite
10. polite
11. polite
12. impolite (maybe he didn't hear her??)

GREETING PEERS

IV-31   YOUR OWN GREETINGS

Objective: The student will greet others appropriately.

Directions

To the teacher: Now that the student has had some experience with identifying polite greetings, he has an opportunity to write or tell what he might say to greet others politely. The student is presented with situations in which a child is greeting a bus driver, a teacher, and a peer. Each student is to write (or tell) what he or she would say in that child's place. Ideas and comments should be shared with the class.

To the student: Now that you know about polite ways to greet people, you are going to have a chance to tell us what *you* would say to greet others. There are three pictures on this sheet—in each picture, a child is saying something to a bus driver, a teacher, and someone else in the class. Pretend you are that child and write or tell what you would be saying. The rest of us will tell you if you were polite (in our opinion!).

Answers

Responses will vary, but should suggest politeness!

YOUR OWN GREETINGS

1.

2.

3.

IV-32   SWEET PARTINGS

Objective: The student will part with others appropriately.

Directions

To the teacher: The "flip side" of greeting someone politely is leaving that person politely when parting. Students on this sheet will identify which of the partings listed are polite and which are not. Discuss briefly why it is important to part politely (for example, you may not see that person in a while and you want to leave a good impression) and why the impolite partings are not appropriate to use.

To the student: When you leave someone, you should be just as polite as when you first meet or greet him or her. We are going to be talking about polite ways to leave, or to part, with someone. Here are some examples. I want you to tell me whether this parting is polite, and if it is not, why it isn't. Maybe you can think of something polite to say instead. Let's hear your ideas.

Answers

1. polite
2. impolite
3. impolite (expressing an emotion, but not appropriate at this time!)
4. polite
5. polite
6. impolite
7. impolite (conveys feeling that his needs are more important than yours)
8. polite
9. polite (it's not verbal, but it's a polite gesture)
10. impolite (nonverbal impolite gesture)

SWEET PARTINGS

Which of these are nice ways to say goodbye to someone?
Circle the nice ways.
Put an X on the ways that are not very nice.

1. goodbye!

2. Blaaaaaaaa!

3. I'm glad I don't have to see you again for a few hours!

4. See you later!

5. Bye-bye! Have a nice evening!

6. Good riddance!

7. Get out of my way!

8. Bye, Sally!

9. (Wave)

10. (Poke in the back)

IV-33 SAY GOODBYE NOW

Objective: The student will part with others appropriately.

Directions

To the teacher: On this page, the student will identify with a child in three situations—parting with a peer, the teacher, and the bus driver. In each situation, he is to write or tell an appropriate parting for each child.

To the student: You are going to look at children in three pictures. In the first one, a girl and a boy are leaving each other; in the second, a boy is leaving his teacher; and in the third, a girl is getting off her bus. For each situation, I would like you to write or tell what you could say politely to leave someone if you were in that situation. Let's share our comments with others and see if we can come up with some polite partings!

Answers

Responses will vary, but typical responses may include:

1. Goodbye, Tommy. Goodbye, Sally.
2. See you tomorrow, Miss Jones.
3. Thanks for the good ride, Mr. Benton!

SAY GOODBYE NOW

1.

2.

3.

IV-34   GOOD READERS

Objective: The student will interact appropriately with peers and adults in a variety of settings.

Directions

To the teacher: The next five worksheets deal with appropriate behavior under different circumstances in classroom settings. In each setting, appropriate behavior may be defined differently. The student is to discuss the setting, talk about what is usually considered appropriate (perhaps in your own classroom), and decide whether this is an appropriate setting to engage in the behaviors listed on the sheet. The student is to circle *yes* or *no,* depending on the situation. An additional section discusses the child who has a question while the class is in that setting. Depending on your own procedures and class rules, the answers to those questions will be relative. Nevertheless, this may be a good time to discuss what you would like your students to do under those conditions.

To the student: We are going to pretend that you and your reading group are at the back table. While this is going on, I want you to think about whether it would be a good time to do some other things. For example, would this be a good time to start reading the next story in your book? (probably not). Why not? (couldn't listen to teacher at the same time).

(Continue in this manner, discussing the appropriateness of the listed behaviors.)

Answers

Responses may vary according to the teacher's class rules, but possible responses are:

1. no
2. yes
3. no
4. no
5. yes
6. no
7. no
8. yes
9. no (unless it's about the reading assignment)
10. no

GOOD READERS

Your reading group is at the back table with the teacher. The teacher is calling on different children to read out loud.

Is this a good time to

1. start reading the next story in your book?	yes	no
2. wait quietly until it is your turn?	yes	no
3. get up to get your pencil?	yes	no
4. make a bookmark?	yes	no
5. listen to the other children read?	yes	no
6. ask the teacher how old she is?	yes	no
7. laugh at the children who can't read well?	yes	no

If you have a question you should

8. raise your hand to ask it.	yes	no
9. ask when it is your turn to read.	yes	no
10. ask when your reading group is finished.	yes	no

IV-35 GOOD EATERS

Objective: The student will interact appropriately with peers and adults in a variety of settings.

Directions

To the teacher: As with the previous worksheet, the student is to decide whether the listed behaviors are appropriate for the highlighted setting—in this case, the lunchroom. Have students indicate their choices by circling the *yes* or *no* after the question. Discuss why a behavior may not be appropriate under those circumstances and what a more appropriate behavior would be.

To the student: This time I want you to pretend that our class is in the lunchroom. The rules for the lunchroom in this school (which may or may not be the same as for your school) state that if a student has a problem, he or she should get the attention of one of the teachers on duty by raising a hand. Let's think about some of the things students might want to do during lunchtime and decide whether this would be a good time to do it. Then we'll talk about why it's a good idea or why it isn't.

Answers

Responses may vary according to the lunchroom procedure of your school, but suggested responses are:

1. no
2. yes (if done quietly)
3. no
4. no
5. yes

6. could be yes or no
7. could be yes or no
8. no
9. yes
10. no

GOOD EATERS

Your class is in the lunchroom. Two teachers are on lunch duty, which means you should ask them to help you with problems during lunch time. You are supposed to raise your hand if you need help with lunch problems.

Is this a good time to

1. try to throw your silverware into the trash?	yes	no
2. talk to your friend about what you will do this weekend?	yes	no
3. sing?	yes	no
4. arm wrestle?	yes	no
5. talk about what you will do at recess?	yes	no
6. ask if you can use the restroom?	yes	no
7. ask if you can go get a drink?	yes	no

If you have a question you should

8. get out of your seat and ask a teacher.	yes	no
9. raise your hand and wait for help.	yes	no
10. go back to your room and find your teacher.	yes	no

IV-36 GOOD RESTROOMERS

Objective: The student will interact appropriately with peers and adults in a variety of settings.

Directions

To the teacher: The student will decide whether the behaviors provided on the worksheet are appropriate or inappropriate for the restroom setting. Discuss your class rules relative to using the restroom. In this example, the teacher's directions were to be quiet and quick. Have the student circle *yes* or *no* according to his or her decision about the appropriateness of the listed behavior. Discuss reasons for the responses.

To the student: In this example, the teacher has sent the children to the restroom. She told them to be quiet and quick. What do you think she meant by that? I want you to pretend that you are a member of that class and circle *yes* or *no* after the list of behaviors that you might want to do. Then let's talk about why it may or may not be a good idea to do that in the restroom.

Answers

Responses may vary according to the school's restroom procedures, but suggested responses are:

1. no
2. yes
3. yes
4. no
5. no
6. yes
7. no
8. no (wait until you're back in the room—unless it's immediately relevant!)
9. yes (probably)
10. yes

GOOD RESTROOMERS

It is time for your class to use the restroom. The teacher told your class to be quiet and quick.

Is this a good time to

1. practice your cheerleading yells?	yes	no
2. wash your hands?	yes	no
3. comb your hair?	yes	no
4. play tag?	yes	no
5. throw water on someone you don't like?	yes	no
6. use the restroom?	yes	no
7. write on the bathroom walls with a marker?	yes	no

If you have a question you should

8. run down the hall and ask your teacher.	yes	no
9. wait until you are back in the classroom.	yes	no
10. ask a friend quietly.	yes	no

IV-37 GOOD BOOKWORMS

Objective: The student will interact appropriately with peers and adults in a variety of settings.

Directions

To the teacher: The student is to decide the appropriateness of listed behaviors for when the class is in the library. The student should circle *yes* or *no* following the behavior to indicate whether it should be done in the library. Discuss reasons why that behavior may not be appropriate at that time.

To the student: This time you are going to pretend that your class is in the library. The librarian is reading the class a story about horses. Now I want you to think about the behaviors listed on the sheet and decide whether they would be good things to do during library time. Circle *yes* if you think it would be OK; circle *no* if this would not be a good time.

Answers

Responses may vary according to the library procedure of your school, but suggested responses are:

1. no
2. no
3. yes
4. no
5. no
6. yes
7. no
8. yes
9. no
10. no (it may still disturb others)

GOOD BOOKWORMS

Your class is in the library. The librarian is reading the class a story about horses.

Is this a good time to

1. raise your hand and ask to go get a drink?   yes   no
2. talk to your neighbor about a horse you used to ride?   yes   no
3. sit very quietly and listen to the story?   yes   no
4. sharpen your pencil?   yes   no
5. start talking about what you will do this weekend?   yes   no
6. learn something about horses?   yes   no
7. tilt your chair backward and see how far you can go without
   tipping it over?   yes   no

If you have a question you should

8. ask it when the teacher has finished reading.   yes   no
9. never ask it.   yes   no
10. ask someone who is sitting next to you.   yes   no

IV-38   GOOD PLAYERS

Objective: The student will interact appropriately with peers and adults in a variety of settings.

Directions

To the teacher: The student is to decide the appropriateness of listed behaviors for when the class is outside or having recess. The student should circle *yes* or *no* following the behavior to indicate whether it is an appropriate behavior for the playground. Discuss reasons why that behavior may or may not be appropriate at that time.

To the student: This time you are going to pretend that your class is outside during recess. The rules for being outside are: (1) stay on the playground; (2) no fighting; and (3) play by the rules if you play a game. Now I want you to think about the behaviors listed on the sheet and decide whether they would be good things to do during recess or on the playground. Circle *yes* if you think it would be OK; circle *no* if this would not be a good time.

Answers

Responses may vary according to the playground rules of your school, but suggested responses are:

1. no
2. yes
3. yes
4. no
5. no
6. no
7. no
8. no
9. yes
10. no
11. yes
12. no
13. yes

GOOD PLAYERS

Your class is on the playground for recess. Your teacher is in the room while another teacher is outside, watching the classes. The playground rules are: (1) stay on the playground; (2) no fighting; and (3) play by the rules if you play a game.

Is this a good time to

1. ask if you can go back in to finish your lunch?	yes	no
2. jump rope?	yes	no
3. ask a friend to play kickball with you?	yes	no
4. go inside to finish cleaning out your desk?	yes	no
5. stick your tongue out at someone you don't like?	yes	no
6. ask if you can visit your grandmother who lives across the street?	yes	no
7. take all of the bases so the boys can't play baseball?	yes	no
8. quit in the middle of a game of kickball?	yes	no
9. practice cheerleading?	yes	no

If you have a question, you should

10. go inside and find your teacher.	yes	no
11. ask the teacher who is outside.	yes	no
12. call your mother.	yes	no
13. ask the teacher who is outside if you can call your mother.	yes	no

IV-39   GOOD RIDERS

Objective: The student will interact appropriately with peers and adults in a variety of settings.

Directions

To the teacher: The student is to decide the appropriateness of listed behaviors for when they are riding the school bus. The student should circle *yes* or *no* following the behavior to indicate whether it is appropriate on the bus. Discuss reasons why that behavior may or may not be appropriate for that situation.

To the student: Now you are going to pretend you are riding the school bus. The rules for riding the bus are: (1) sit in the same seat; (2) don't switch seats; (3) don't stand up or move while the bus is moving. Now I want you to look at the behaviors listed on the sheet and decide whether they would be OK to do on the bus. Circle *yes* if you think it would be OK; circle *no* if you think it would not be the right time to do it. Then we will talk about your answers.

Answers

Responses may vary according to your school's bus riding procedures, but suggested responses are:

1. no
2. yes
3. no
4. no (the bus is moving)
5. could be yes or no
6. yes
7. no
8. yes
9. yes (if appropriate question for school)

NAME _____   DATE _____

GOOD RIDERS

You are on the bus, going to school. Your bus driver makes everyone sit in the same seat and no one is allowed to switch seats. No one is supposed to stand up or move around while the bus is moving.

Is this a good time to

1. ask your bus driver to go faster?   yes   no
2. talk to the person sitting next to you?   yes   no
3. talk to someone 10 seats away?   yes   no
4. ask the bus driver to help you open the window?   yes   no
5. tell everyone that it is your friend's birthday and you want everyone
   to sing "Happy Birthday"?   yes   no
6. say "good morning" to the bus driver?   yes   no

If you have a question, you should

7. ask the bus driver to take you home so you can ask your mother.   yes   no
8. ask your bus driver when the bus is stopped.   yes   no
9. wait until you get to school.   yes   no

ENRICHMENT ACTIVITIES

MY VACATION ON EARTH (IV-1) can be extended by having students write their own "Rizbo" stories in which they leave out certain words (probably nouns) and insert clues. They can read their stories out loud to the class and have others guess what the missing words are.

WHAT'S IN THE BAG (IV-5) can easily be extended by having students actually bring in a small paper bag with something in it. The students can rattle their bags and the contents before giving clues that are descriptive of their object.

FACTS AND OPINIONS (IV-6 through IV-9) can be extended to encompass daily activities. For example, ask the students to listen for three opinions about the playground equipment during recess time. Have them listen to the nightly news program for three facts about their community. This could also be done using a newspaper or other written medium. Taking a poll is an enjoyable way for students to talk to other students about current school events, the cafeteria food, or the principal.

THE NEW STUDENT (IV-13) can be a role-playing activity that can give students insight into what it feels like to be new in a situation and need to find out how procedures operate. Students can take turns being the new student and being the explainers.

WHAT DID YOU DO TODAY? (IV-14) can be turned into a week-long activity in which the students record what they do and their evaluation of it on a daily (or an hourly?) basis. This can provide lots of discussion opportunities.

Creating stories from pictures (**Activities IV-16 through IV-19**) can also be accomplished by using photographs or observing school activities (for example, children on the playground at recess). The stories can be collected and compiled into a book to be sent home to parents. In some cases, children who are adept at drawing may wish to submit a picture for the entire class to write about.

NANCY'S PROBLEM (IV-20) and the following problem-solving activities lend themselves to role-playing situations. Students can take part in small groups to portray the situation, with the student in the main role sometimes doing the *wrong* thing. Student observers can discuss the performance afterwards, giving opinions about the appropriateness of the handling of the problem.

MAY I? (IV-23) can be played as a game, in which the students are (temporarily) not allowed to do *anything* (except involuntary motor functions like breathing) without first asking permission of the leader (teacher or another student). They will have to ask things like: "May I get out of my seat? May I give Billy his book? May I open the book? Do you mind if I sharpen my pencil? Could I use my pencil to write my name?"

HOW I FEEL TODAY (IV-25) and other activities about emotions can be role-played by students. Situations can be devised in which a student is made to feel sadness, anger, or some other emotion. At this time, emotions beyond the four mentioned in the worksheet may be discussed. Students may want to make booklets or posters that have pictures of people expressing different emotions. Short stories could be written using some of the posters and shared with the class.

GREETING PEOPLE activities (IV-28 through IV-31) and PARTINGS (IV-32 through IV-33) can be made into real-life activities. Have the children record for one week as many different greetings and partings that they hear as possible. Some children may want to take the bus setting; others may want to listen in the classroom; others may take a poll of what is the first thing students say when they walk in the door at home. These results can be compiled, graphed, role-played, or made into posters.